50 Christian Arguments For Anarchism

By James Hosie

1

Anarchist Christians often assert that the only legitimate authority is divine, rooted in their interpretation of biblical teachings. This perspective challenges the legitimacy of human institutions, arguing that they are inherently fallible and susceptible to corruption. Here's a closer look at this argument:

1. **Divine Sovereignty:**
   - Anarchist Christians maintain that God is the ultimate authority, and any attempt to establish authority apart from or in contradiction to the divine is fundamentally flawed. This belief is grounded in the understanding that God's sovereignty transcends human constructs.

2. **Fallibility of Human Institutions:**
   - Drawing from a theological standpoint, these Christians argue that human institutions, be they political, social, or economic, are inherently fallible due to the fallen nature of humanity. Flaws, biases, and

corruption can infiltrate these structures, leading to injustices and abuses of power.

3. **Biblical Critique of Earthly Authorities:**
   - Anarchist Christians often reference biblical passages that caution against putting trust in human rulers or earthly authorities. They may point to instances where rulers deviate from divine principles, emphasizing the need for skepticism towards worldly systems.

4. **Corruption in Power Structures:**
   - This perspective underscores the corrupting influence of power when concentrated in human institutions. Anarchist Christians may argue that hierarchical structures tend to centralize power, leading to exploitation, oppression, and moral compromise.

5. **Moral Autonomy and Divine Law:**
   - Advocates of this viewpoint stress the importance of moral autonomy guided by divine law. They contend that individuals

should be directly accountable to God's moral standards rather than relying on human authorities to interpret and enforce ethical principles.

6. **Rejecting a Human-Centric Authority:**
   - Anarchist Christians may reject the notion of placing ultimate authority in the hands of fallible humans, asserting that such an arrangement contradicts the acknowledgment of God as the supreme and infallible source of authority.

7. **Call for Decentralization:**
   - Advocates for divine authority often support decentralized, community-based decision-making processes. They argue that localized and participatory structures are more aligned with a humble acknowledgment of human limitations and a recognition of God's ultimate authority.

8. **Distrust of Power Structures:**
   - This perspective involves a fundamental distrust of human-made power structures, expressing concerns about the potential for

such structures to become instruments of oppression and manipulation rather than channels of justice and righteousness.

In essence, the argument put forth by Anarchist Christians regarding the exclusive legitimacy of divine authority stems from a deep theological conviction that human institutions, due to their fallibility and susceptibility to corruption, should not be considered the ultimate source of authority in matters of governance and morality.

2

Christian anarchists, drawing inspiration from the teachings of Jesus, often advocate for a societal framework grounded in radical love and nonviolence. Their position asserts that coercive institutions contradict the core principles espoused by Jesus and promotes an alternative vision for communal living. Here's an exploration of this perspective:

1. **Central Tenets of Jesus' Teaching:**

- Christian anarchists start by emphasizing the central tenets of Jesus' teachings, such as love, compassion, forgiveness, and nonviolence. They argue that these principles form the foundation of a just and harmonious society.

2. **Radical Love as a Guiding Principle:**
   - At the heart of the Christian anarchist perspective is the emphasis on radical love, a love that goes beyond conventional boundaries. They see this as a transformative force capable of breaking down societal divisions and fostering genuine community.

3. **Nonviolent Resistance:**
   - Building on Jesus' advocacy for nonviolent resistance, Christian anarchists reject the use of force or coercion in addressing societal issues. They believe in confronting injustice through nonviolent means, even in the face of oppression.

4. **Critique of Coercive Institutions:**
   - Advocates of Christian anarchism argue that coercive institutions, such as the state

and its enforcement mechanisms, inherently rely on force and violence. They contend that such structures stand in stark contrast to Jesus' teachings, which promote love, reconciliation, and turning the other cheek.

5. **Rejecting the Sword:**
   - Christian anarchists often reference Jesus' statement, "Put your sword back into its place," as a symbolic rejection of violent solutions. They interpret this as a clear directive against the use of force to achieve societal goals.

6. **Alternative Models of Governance:**
   - Proponents of Christian anarchism propose alternative models of governance that prioritize voluntary cooperation and consensus-building over hierarchical structures. They believe in the capacity of communities to self-organize without the need for external coercion.

7. **Community-Based Decision Making:**
   - Emphasizing Jesus' teachings on community and service, Christian anarchists

advocate for decentralized decision-making processes within communities. This approach fosters a sense of shared responsibility and mutual aid.

8. **Seeking Justice Through Love:**
   - Christian anarchists argue that true justice can only be achieved through love and compassion, not through punitive measures or the threat of force. They envision a society where individuals are motivated by a genuine concern for the well-being of others.

9. **Living Out the Sermon on the Mount:**
   - The Sermon on the Mount, with its emphasis on humility, peacemaking, and love for enemies, serves as a blueprint for Christian anarchists. They see these teachings as a call to embody an alternative way of life that challenges existing power structures.

10. **Toward a Kingdom of God on Earth:**
   - The ultimate goal for Christian anarchists is to work towards the establishment of a "Kingdom of God on Earth," characterized by love, justice, and nonviolence. They believe

that embracing these principles is essential for realizing a more just and compassionate society.

In summary, Christian anarchists draw from Jesus' teachings to advocate for a society founded on radical love and nonviolence, rejecting coercive institutions in favor of alternative, community-based models that reflect the transformative power of Christian principles.

3

Certain Christian anarchists find inspiration in the simple and communal lifestyle that Jesus is believed to have lived, and they argue that hierarchical structures and systems are inconsistent with the teachings of Christ. Here's an exploration of this perspective:

1. **Jesus' Simple Lifestyle:**
   - Christian anarchists who embrace this perspective point to Jesus' own lifestyle, which is often depicted as humble and characterized by minimalism. They argue that

he eschewed material wealth and worldly possessions, emphasizing a focus on spiritual values and compassionate living.

2. **Communal Living in the Early Christian Communities:**
   - These Christian anarchists draw inspiration from the early Christian communities described in the New Testament, where believers are portrayed as sharing resources and living in communal harmony. They see this as a model for a society based on cooperation and mutual support.

3. **Rejecting Accumulation of Wealth:**
   - Advocates of this viewpoint assert that Jesus' teachings include a strong critique of the accumulation of wealth and the pursuit of material possessions. They believe that hierarchical structures often perpetuate economic disparities and go against the spirit of Christ's teachings on simplicity.

4. **Equality and Brotherhood:**

  - Christian anarchists argue that hierarchical structures inherently foster inequality and a lack of brotherhood, contrary to Jesus' emphasis on love for one another and the notion of all individuals as children of God. They seek to promote a sense of equality and solidarity among people.

5. **Challenging Status and Power:**
   - Hierarchical systems, according to Christian anarchists, can perpetuate a concentration of power and status that contradicts the servant leadership model presented by Jesus. They advocate for a rejection of worldly hierarchies in favor of a more egalitarian and inclusive approach.

6. **Servant Leadership:**
   - Embracing the concept of servant leadership emphasized in Jesus' teachings, these Christian anarchists argue that leaders should embody humility and a willingness to serve rather than enforce authority from a position of power.

7. **Community-Based Decision Making:**

- In alignment with the communal aspects of Jesus' life, Christian anarchists often promote community-based decision-making processes where individuals collectively participate in shaping the direction of their communities. This is seen as a departure from hierarchical decision-making structures.

8. **Critique of Institutionalized Religion:**
   - Some Christian anarchists extend their critique beyond political and economic hierarchies to institutionalized religion. They argue that rigid ecclesiastical structures can deviate from the communal and egalitarian aspects of Jesus' teachings.

9. **Living Simply as a Form of Witness:**
   - Christian anarchists who emulate Jesus' simple lifestyle view it as a powerful form of witness to the world. They believe that by living modestly and communally, they can embody the values of the Kingdom of God and challenge societal norms centered around materialism and individualism.

10. **A Call to Authentic Discipleship:**

- For these Christian anarchists, adopting a simple and communal lifestyle is viewed as a commitment to authentic discipleship, aligning one's life with the radical message of Jesus and challenging societal structures that deviate from these principles.

In essence, the belief that hierarchical structures contradict the teachings of Christ is rooted in a desire to emulate Jesus' simplicity, promote communal living, and challenge systems that perpetuate inequality and a departure from the core values of Christian teachings.

4

Christian anarchists often advocate for a societal framework grounded in mutual aid and voluntary cooperation, drawing inspiration from biblical principles that emphasize caring for one another and fostering strong, supportive communities. Here's an exploration of this perspective:

1. **Biblical Foundations of Mutual Aid:**

- Christian anarchists point to various biblical passages that underscore the importance of mutual aid and caring for one another. Scriptures such as "Love your neighbor as yourself" (Mark 12:31) and the early Christian community's practice of sharing resources (Acts 2:44-45) serve as foundations for their advocacy.

2. **Voluntary Cooperation Over Coercion:**
   - Emphasizing the voluntariness of cooperation, Christian anarchists reject coercive structures and argue that individuals should willingly come together to meet collective needs. They contend that a society based on voluntary cooperation is more aligned with biblical principles than one relying on force or compulsion.

3. **The Golden Rule:**
   - The Golden Rule, "Do unto others as you would have them do unto you" (Matthew 7:12), is central to the Christian anarchist perspective. They believe that this principle calls for a society in which individuals

voluntarily contribute to the well-being of others, fostering a sense of reciprocity and empathy.

4. **Caring for the Least Among Us:**
   - Christian anarchists often reference Jesus' teachings about caring for the least among us, as outlined in the parable of the sheep and the goats (Matthew 25:31-46). They argue that a society built on mutual aid prioritizes the needs of the marginalized and vulnerable, reflecting Christ's concern for the marginalized.

5. **Rejecting Materialism and Consumerism:**
   - Advocates of this viewpoint critique the materialistic and consumerist aspects of modern society, arguing that they run counter to biblical teachings on contentment, simplicity, and sharing. They advocate for an economic system that prioritizes the well-being of all over the accumulation of wealth.

6. **Communal Living as a Biblical Ideal:**

- Christian anarchists often look to the early Christian communities described in the New Testament as a model for communal living. They highlight passages that describe believers sharing possessions and supporting one another (Acts 4:32-35), viewing this as an ideal for a society based on mutual aid.

7. **Stewardship of Resources:**
   - Stewardship principles found in the Bible influence Christian anarchists' views on resource management. They believe in responsible stewardship, using resources wisely and ensuring that all members of society have access to what they need for a dignified life.

8. **Building Strong, Supportive Communities:**
   - The emphasis on mutual aid extends to the idea of building strong, supportive communities. Christian anarchists envision a society where individuals voluntarily work together to address each other's needs, creating a sense of belonging and shared responsibility.

9. **Nonviolent Solutions to Conflict:**
   - Mutual aid, for Christian anarchists, extends to conflict resolution. They advocate for nonviolent solutions and restorative justice, guided by biblical principles that promote reconciliation and forgiveness over punitive measures.

10. **Witness to Christian Love:**
   - In advocating for a society based on mutual aid, Christian anarchists see it as a tangible expression of Christian love in action. They believe that such a society would serve as a powerful witness to the transformative nature of Christ's teachings.

In summary, Christian anarchists argue for a societal structure rooted in mutual aid and voluntary cooperation, aligning with biblical principles of love, care for one another, and the formation of strong, supportive communities. This perspective seeks to embody Christian values in the way society is organized and individuals interact.

5

Anarchist Christians often highlight the violent nature of states, contending that a true Christian society should reject coercive institutions and instead embrace peaceful and just alternatives. Here's an exploration of this perspective:

1. **Nonviolence in Christian Ethics:**
   - Anarchist Christians draw on the broader Christian ethical tradition, particularly the teachings of Jesus, which emphasize nonviolence, love for enemies, and turning the other cheek (Matthew 5:38-48). They argue that the inherently violent nature of states contradicts these foundational principles.

2. **Critique of War and Aggression:**
   - Pointing to historical instances of war and aggression undertaken by states, anarchist Christians critique the use of force as a means of achieving political objectives. They contend that war and violence are

incompatible with the Christian call for peace and reconciliation.

3. **State as an Instrument of Violence:**
   - Anarchist Christians view the state as an institution that often relies on coercion, punishment, and violence to maintain order and enforce its authority. They argue that such means of control are fundamentally at odds with the teachings of Christ.

4. **Alternative Models of Governance:**
   - Advocates of this viewpoint propose alternative models of governance that prioritize nonviolent conflict resolution and cooperation. They believe that a society based on mutual consent and voluntary cooperation can address disputes without resorting to state-sanctioned violence.

5. **Rejecting State-Sponsored Injustice:**
   - Anarchist Christians critique state-sponsored injustices, such as discrimination, oppression, and systemic violence. They argue that true Christian principles call for

active resistance against structures that perpetuate inequality and harm.

6. **Pacifism as a Christian Virtue:**
   - Pacifism is often considered a virtue by anarchist Christians, influenced by the belief that Jesus' teachings reject violence in all its forms. They assert that a commitment to pacifism is a logical extension of Christian love and the pursuit of justice.

7. **Embracing Restorative Justice:**
   - Anarchist Christians advocate for restorative justice principles, emphasizing reconciliation, restitution, and rehabilitation over punitive measures. They argue that a Christian society should prioritize healing and transformation rather than punitive consequences.

8. **Modeling Christ's Sacrificial Love:**
   - The sacrificial love demonstrated by Jesus on the cross is a central theme for anarchist Christians. They argue that this selfless love should guide societal structures, promoting

compassion, forgiveness, and a commitment to the well-being of all.

9. **Pilgrimage Toward a Peaceful Kingdom:**
   - Anarchist Christians see their commitment to nonviolence as part of a broader pilgrimage toward the establishment of a peaceful Kingdom of God on Earth. They envision a society where individuals work collaboratively for the common good without relying on coercive state apparatus.

10. **Active Peacemaking:**
   - Anarchist Christians view themselves as active peacemakers, engaging in efforts to address root causes of conflict, promote dialogue, and create conditions conducive to justice and reconciliation. They argue that such efforts align with the Christian mission to be instruments of peace.

In summary, anarchist Christians critique the violent nature of states, asserting that a true Christian society should reject coercive institutions. They advocate for alternative models rooted in nonviolence, justice, and the transformative principles found in the teachings of Jesus.

6

Christian anarchists often draw from biblical passages to argue against the establishment of earthly kingdoms, emphasizing the transient and flawed nature of human political structures. Here's an exploration of this perspective:

1. **The Temptation in the Wilderness:**
   - Christian anarchists may point to the temptation of Jesus in the wilderness (Matthew 4:8-10) where Satan offers him all the kingdoms of the world. Jesus responds by affirming the worship of God alone, suggesting a rejection of earthly kingdoms and their potentially corrupting influence.

2. **Jesus' Response to Pilate:**
   - Christian anarchists might reference Jesus' response to Pontius Pilate's question about whether he is a king. Jesus clarifies that his

kingdom is not of this world (John 18:36), indicating a distinction between the divine realm and the flawed political structures of human society.

3. **God as the Ultimate Ruler:**
   - Emphasizing biblical passages that declare God as the ultimate ruler and sovereign authority, Christian anarchists argue that placing trust in earthly kingdoms undermines the acknowledgment of God's supremacy (Psalm 103:19; Daniel 4:17).

4. **Warnings Against Earthly Kings:**
   - The Old Testament contains warnings about the consequences of having earthly kings, as seen in God's caution to the Israelites in 1 Samuel 8. The desire for a human king is portrayed as a rejection of God's direct rule, and Christian anarchists may use this narrative to caution against relying on human political structures.

5. **The Transience of Earthly Power:**
   - Christian anarchists might draw attention to passages that highlight the fleeting nature

of human power and kingdoms. Verses such as Isaiah 40:15 and Daniel 2:44 emphasize the temporal and transient nature of political structures, suggesting that earthly kingdoms are subject to change and decay.

6. **The Kingdom of God Within:**
   - Drawing from Jesus' teaching that the Kingdom of God is within individuals (Luke 17:21), Christian anarchists argue that the focus should be on internal spiritual transformation rather than the external pursuit of political power. This perspective challenges the notion of establishing earthly kingdoms as the ultimate goal.

7. **Fallen Human Nature and Corruption:**
   - Christian anarchists may reference the biblical concept of the fallen nature of humanity to argue that any human-created political structure is susceptible to corruption and moral compromise (Jeremiah 17:9; Romans 3:23).

8. **The Tower of Babel:**

- The story of the Tower of Babel in Genesis 11 is often cited by Christian anarchists. The narrative illustrates the potential pitfalls of human attempts to build grand structures and establish powerful kingdoms without proper regard for God's guidance.

9. **Jesus' Rejection of Worldly Glory:**
   - Christian anarchists may highlight instances where Jesus rejected worldly glory and power, such as when he resisted the temptation to rule over earthly kingdoms and consistently advocated for humility and servant leadership (Matthew 20:25-28; Mark 10:42-45).

10. **A Call to Seek the Kingdom of God:**
    - Christian anarchists argue that the central focus should be on seeking the Kingdom of God rather than aspiring to build earthly kingdoms (Matthew 6:33). This perspective aligns with the idea that the ultimate goal is spiritual and involves a commitment to divine principles over human political structures.

In summary, Christian anarchists use biblical passages to argue against the creation of earthly kingdoms, emphasizing the transient and flawed nature of human political structures. They contend that a genuine Christian perspective should prioritize the acknowledgment of God's sovereignty and the pursuit of spiritual values over the establishment of earthly political realms.

7

Christian anarchists, inspired by the concept of servant leadership, advocate for a model where leaders are chosen based on their willingness to serve rather than obtaining positions through hierarchical authority. Here's an exploration of this perspective:

1. **Jesus as the Ultimate Servant Leader:**
   - Christian anarchists draw inspiration from Jesus, who exemplified servant leadership throughout his ministry. They highlight instances such as the washing of the disciples' feet (John 13:1-17) as a powerful demonstration of leading through service.

2. **Biblical Mandate for Humble Leadership:**
   - Christian anarchists point to biblical teachings that emphasize humility and the rejection of positions of power. Verses like Philippians 2:3-8 call believers to emulate Christ's humility, providing a foundation for the rejection of hierarchical power structures.

3. **Jesus' Teaching on Leadership:**
   - Christian anarchists may reference Jesus' teachings on leadership, particularly his contrast between worldly leadership and the leadership expected among his followers. He emphasizes servant leadership, stating that the greatest among them should be the servant of all (Matthew 20:25-28).

4. **Leadership as a Form of Service:**
   - Christian anarchists argue that leadership should be viewed as a form of service rather than a means of control or authority. They assert that leaders should actively work to meet the needs of those they lead, fostering a

sense of community and shared responsibility.

5. **Rejecting Coercive Authority:**
   - Embracing the servant leadership model, Christian anarchists reject the idea of leaders exercising coercive authority. They contend that leadership should be based on voluntary cooperation and the willingness of individuals to follow those who genuinely serve the common good.

6. **Consensus-Building and Collaboration:**
   - Servant leadership, as envisioned by Christian anarchists, involves consensus-building and collaboration. Leaders are expected to facilitate discussions, listen to the concerns of the community, and work toward decisions that reflect the collective will rather than imposing their own authority.

7. **Equality Among Believers:**
   - Christian anarchists argue that the servant leadership model promotes equality among believers, dismantling hierarchical

distinctions. They believe that all members of the community have unique gifts and contributions, and leadership should emerge organically based on service rather than imposed titles.

8. **Empowering Others:**
   - Servant leaders, according to this perspective, prioritize empowering others rather than seeking personal power. They aim to develop the potential of those they lead, fostering a community where everyone is encouraged to contribute and take on leadership roles as needed.

9. **Moral Authority over Positional Authority:**
   - Christian anarchists assert that leaders should derive their authority from moral character and the willingness to serve rather than relying on positional authority. This approach fosters a leadership style rooted in trust and shared values.

10. **Imitating Christ's Sacrificial Love:**

- Servant leadership, for Christian anarchists, involves imitating Christ's sacrificial love. Leaders are called to make personal sacrifices for the well-being of others, prioritizing the needs of the community over personal gain or status.

In summary, Christian anarchists advocate for a model of leadership grounded in the principles of servant leadership, where individuals are chosen based on their willingness to serve and facilitate the well-being of the community. This approach seeks to reflect the humility and sacrificial love modeled by Jesus in his earthly ministry.

8

Christian anarchists often emphasize the importance of free will, asserting that individuals should be free to make choices without the imposition of external authority. This perspective is rooted in theological and ethical considerations that value human autonomy and responsibility. Here's an exploration of this viewpoint:

1. **God-Given Free Will:**
   - Christian anarchists assert that free will is a gift from God, granted to humanity as part of being created in the image of God. They argue that God's intention is for individuals to exercise their free will in making choices that align with moral and spiritual values.

2. **Moral Responsibility and Accountability:**
   - Emphasizing free will, Christian anarchists stress the moral responsibility of individuals for their actions. They argue that genuine moral choices and ethical behavior require the freedom to make decisions without external coercion.

3. **Biblical Recognition of Free Will:**
   - Christian anarchists may refer to biblical passages that recognize and affirm the role of free will in human decision-making. Examples include passages that call for choosing between good and evil, such as Deuteronomy 30:19 and Joshua 24:15.

4. **Rejecting Coercion in Matters of
Faith:**
   - In matters of faith, Christian anarchists
contend that faith and belief should be
voluntary and genuine. They reject the use of
coercion or force in matters of religious
conviction, emphasizing that true faith must
arise from a freely made commitment.

5. **Imitating God's Relationship with
Humanity:**
   - Christian anarchists draw inspiration from
the relationship between God and humanity,
pointing out that God does not coerce or force
individuals into obedience. They argue that
humans should imitate God's approach by
respecting each other's free will.

6. **Nonviolent Principles:**
   - Advocates of free will within Christian
anarchism often align with nonviolent
principles. They argue that imposing external
authority infringes on the nonviolent spirit
promoted by Jesus, who respected
individuals' choices and encouraged peaceful,
voluntary cooperation.

7. **Community Based on Voluntary Cooperation:**
   - Christian anarchists envision a community based on voluntary cooperation, where individuals freely choose to contribute to the well-being of the community without external coercion. This aligns with their understanding of free will as a foundation for genuine community engagement.

8. **Resisting Authoritarian Structures:**
   - Christian anarchists critique authoritarian structures, whether political or religious, as infringing upon individual free will. They argue that such structures can stifle personal autonomy and inhibit the expression of God-given agency.

9. **Empowering Individuals:**
   - The emphasis on free will is coupled with a desire to empower individuals. Christian anarchists believe that acknowledging and respecting free will allows individuals to take active roles in shaping their own lives and communities.

10. **Building a Just Society Without Coercion:**
   - Christian anarchists envision a just society where individuals voluntarily participate in creating and maintaining order without the need for external coercion. They argue that true justice can only be achieved when individuals are free to make choices guided by moral principles.

In summary, Christian anarchists stress the importance of free will, contending that individuals should have the autonomy to make choices without the imposition of external authority. This perspective aligns with a vision of communities and societies built on voluntary cooperation, respect for personal autonomy, and adherence to moral and ethical principles.

9

Christian anarchists who emphasize Jesus' teaching that the Kingdom of God is within individuals often argue for a decentralized and individualized approach to spirituality and community. This perspective places a strong emphasis on personal responsibility, autonomy, and the direct connection between individuals and their understanding of God. Here's an exploration of this viewpoint:

1. **The Kingdom of God Within:**
   - Christian anarchists draw from Jesus' teaching, particularly the statement that "the Kingdom of God is within you" (Luke 17:21). They interpret this as an affirmation of the internal, personal nature of spirituality, suggesting that individuals have a direct and personal connection with the divine.

2. **Rejecting External Authority in Spiritual Matters:**
   - Pointing to the idea of the Kingdom of God within, Christian anarchists argue against external religious authority or hierarchical structures in matters of spirituality. They contend that individuals do not need intermediaries to access the divine and that personal revelation is central to a genuine spiritual experience.

3. **Individual Spiritual Autonomy:**
   - Christian anarchists advocate for individual spiritual autonomy, asserting that each person has the capacity and responsibility to discern their own understanding of God and the divine. This approach rejects the imposition of dogma or rigid religious structures that may limit personal exploration and interpretation.

4. **Diverse Spiritual Paths:**
   - In embracing the individualized approach to spirituality, Christian anarchists celebrate the diversity of spiritual paths. They argue that different individuals may experience and express their connection to the divine in unique ways, and a decentralized model allows for this diversity.

5. **Community as Voluntary Association:**
   - Christian anarchists envision communities formed through voluntary association, where individuals come together based on shared values and spiritual journeys rather than strict adherence to a centralized doctrine. This

community model is built on mutual respect for individual differences.

6. **De-emphasizing Institutional Religion:**
   - This perspective often involves a de-emphasis on institutionalized religion, with Christian anarchists expressing skepticism toward religious organizations that wield hierarchical authority. They argue that true spirituality is a personal journey rather than one dictated by institutional structures.

7. **Empowering Each Individual's Spiritual Gifts:**
   - Christian anarchists believe in recognizing and empowering the spiritual gifts that each individual possesses. They argue that a decentralized approach allows individuals to explore and utilize their unique gifts for the benefit of the community without rigid institutional constraints.

8. **Personal Responsibility for Justice and Compassion:**

- The individualized approach extends to social justice and compassion. Christian anarchists assert that individuals, inspired by their personal connection with the divine, should take personal responsibility for addressing social issues and extending compassion to others.

9. **Living Out Christ's Teachings Personally:**
   - Christian anarchists emphasize the personal application of Christ's teachings in daily life. They argue that living out principles such as love, forgiveness, and humility is a direct and personal response to the internal guidance of the Kingdom of God within.

10. **Creating Networks of Autonomous Communities:**
   - In the broader social context, Christian anarchists may envision networks of autonomous communities that come together voluntarily for shared purposes. This decentralized model allows for a diverse

tapestry of spiritual expressions within the larger Christian anarchist framework.

In summary, Christian anarchists pointing to Jesus' teaching on the Kingdom of God within individuals advocate for a decentralized and individualized approach to spirituality and community. This perspective emphasizes personal autonomy, diverse spiritual paths, and voluntary associations based on shared values rather than institutional authority.

10

Christian anarchists who emphasize the responsibility of humans to care for God's creation often argue that a decentralized, community-based approach is more effective in stewarding the environment. Rooted in biblical principles of creation care and stewardship, this perspective emphasizes local engagement, community collaboration, and personal responsibility. Here's an exploration of this viewpoint:

1. **Biblical Mandate for Stewardship:**
   - Christian anarchists stress the biblical mandate for humans to be stewards of God's creation. They often refer to passages such as Genesis 2:15, where humanity is called to "tend and keep" the garden, interpreting it as a directive to responsibly care for the Earth.

2. **Rejecting Exploitative Practices:**
   - Christian anarchists critique industrial and exploitative practices that harm the environment, arguing that these approaches often prioritize profit over responsible stewardship. They advocate for a decentralized model that encourages sustainable practices and local decision-making.

3. **Community-Based Conservation:**
   - Emphasizing the communal aspect of stewardship, Christian anarchists argue that local communities are better equipped to understand and address their unique environmental challenges. They advocate for community-based conservation efforts that

reflect the specific needs and characteristics
of each region.

4. **Building Sustainable Local
Economies:**
   - Christian anarchists promote the idea of
building sustainable local economies that
prioritize environmental well-being. They
argue that a decentralized approach allows
communities to tailor economic practices to
their ecological contexts, fostering harmony
between human activities and the natural
world.

5. **Valuing Biodiversity:**
   - This perspective places a strong emphasis
on valuing biodiversity and the
interconnectedness of ecosystems. Christian
anarchists argue that a decentralized approach
encourages a more intimate understanding of
local ecosystems, promoting practices that
safeguard the diversity of life.

6. **Personal Responsibility for Creation
Care:**

- Individuals, according to Christian anarchists, have a personal responsibility for caring for God's creation. They argue that this responsibility extends beyond merely following environmental regulations and involves actively making choices that contribute to ecological well-being.

7. **Local Solutions to Global Environmental Issues:**
   - Christian anarchists contend that global environmental issues are best addressed through a network of local solutions. They argue that decentralized, community-based initiatives can collectively contribute to a more sustainable and resilient response to challenges like climate change.

8. **Respect for Creation as a Spiritual Duty:**
   - For Christian anarchists, caring for God's creation is not just an environmental concern but also a spiritual duty. They argue that individuals, motivated by their faith, should actively engage in practices that demonstrate

respect for the Earth as a manifestation of God's divine creation.

9. **Promoting Eco-Justice:**
   - Christian anarchists advocate for eco-justice, which involves addressing environmental issues through the lens of social justice. They argue that a community-based approach allows for more equitable distribution of environmental resources and benefits.

10. **Educating and Empowering Local Communities:**
   - This perspective places a significant emphasis on educating and empowering local communities to take ownership of environmental issues. Christian anarchists argue that decentralized initiatives allow for grassroots education, fostering a sense of environmental stewardship at the community level.

In summary, Christian anarchists who emphasize the responsibility of humans to care for God's creation argue for a decentralized, community-based approach to environmental stewardship. This perspective is grounded in biblical principles of stewardship, community collaboration, and a commitment to responsible and sustainable practices that align with ecological well-being.

11

Anarchist Christians contend that human institutions are fallible and prone to corruption, arguing that reliance on such institutions undermines the perfect and just authority of God. Here's an exploration of this perspective:

1. **Fallibility of Human Nature:**
   - Anarchist Christians begin with the understanding that human nature is inherently fallible, susceptible to greed, power-seeking, and moral shortcomings. They draw on theological concepts like original sin to support the view that entrusting too much authority to human institutions risks the propagation of sinful behavior.

2. **Corruption within Power Structures:**
   - Emphasizing the corrupting influence of power, anarchist Christians point to historical and contemporary instances where institutional structures have been marred by abuses of authority, exploitation, and injustice. They argue that power, when concentrated, tends to deviate from ethical principles.

3. **Biblical Warnings Against Earthly Power:**
   - Christian anarchists reference biblical warnings and narratives that caution against placing excessive trust in earthly power. The story of the Tower of Babel in Genesis 11, for instance, is often cited as a cautionary tale about the dangers of centralized human authority and the pursuit of grandiose projects.

4. **Idolatry of Human Systems:**
   - Anarchist Christians contend that an overreliance on human institutions can lead to idolatry, where these structures become the

focal point of authority instead of God. They argue that such idolatry contradicts the principle of acknowledging God as the ultimate and perfect authority.

5. **Rejecting Worldly Hierarchies:**
   - Drawing inspiration from Jesus' teachings, particularly his rebuke of the pursuit of power and status (Matthew 20:25-28), anarchist Christians reject the establishment of hierarchical structures that mimic the world's systems. They assert that such structures can undermine the principles of humility and servant leadership advocated by Jesus.

6. **The Sovereignty of God:**
   - Anarchist Christians emphasize the sovereignty of God as the only perfect and just authority. They argue that human institutions, being inherently flawed, cannot fully embody the divine justice and wisdom that God represents.

7. **Need for Humility and Obedience to God:**

- Advocates of this perspective argue for humility before God and obedience to divine principles over blind allegiance to human institutions. They contend that genuine justice and righteousness can only be achieved by aligning human structures with God's perfect will.

8. **Historical Examples of Injustice:**
   - Pointing to historical examples, anarchist Christians highlight instances where institutions, even those founded with good intentions, have perpetuated injustice and oppression. This historical awareness strengthens their argument against relying on human institutions for ultimate authority.

9. **Embracing a Kingdom-Centric Worldview:**
   - Anarchist Christians adopt a Kingdom-centric worldview, focusing on the establishment of the Kingdom of God on Earth rather than placing undue emphasis on human-created systems. They see this approach as aligning with Jesus' message of

seeking first the Kingdom of God (Matthew 6:33).

10. **A Call for Anarchy in the Original Sense:**
   - Some anarchist Christians frame their perspective as a call for anarchy in its original sense, meaning a society without rulers, where individuals voluntarily follow the divine principles of justice, love, and mutual aid rather than being subject to imperfect human authorities.

In summary, anarchist Christians contend that human institutions, due to their fallibility and susceptibility to corruption, are inadequate substitutes for the perfect and just authority of God. They advocate for a worldview that places God at the center, emphasizing humility, obedience, and a commitment to divine principles over blind trust in human-created structures.

12

Drawing from Jesus' teachings, Christian anarchists emphasize nonviolent resistance to injustice, arguing that coercive institutions contradict the principles of love and nonviolence advocated by Christ. Here's an exploration of this perspective:

1. **Sermon on the Mount:**
   - Christian anarchists often point to Jesus' Sermon on the Mount (Matthew 5-7), where he teaches principles of love, forgiveness, and nonviolence. They see these teachings as foundational to their perspective on resisting injustice without resorting to coercion.

2. **Turning the Other Cheek:**
   - An iconic teaching of Jesus, "turning the other cheek" (Matthew 5:39), is frequently cited by Christian anarchists. They interpret this as a call to reject retaliatory violence and seek nonviolent responses even in the face of injustice.

3. **Love for Enemies:**
   - Jesus' command to "love your enemies and pray for those who persecute you"

(Matthew 5:44) is central to the Christian anarchist perspective. They argue that this teaching challenges the use of force and coercion, advocating for a transformative power of love.

4. **The Golden Rule:**
   - Christian anarchists emphasize the Golden Rule, "Do unto others as you would have them do unto you" (Matthew 7:12), as a guiding principle for nonviolent resistance. They argue that treating others with love and respect aligns with Jesus' teachings and opposes coercive measures.

5. **Jesus' Nonviolent Actions:**
   - Christian anarchists highlight instances in Jesus' life where he demonstrated nonviolent resistance. The cleansing of the temple (Matthew 21:12-13), they argue, is an example of Jesus using symbolic, nonviolent action to challenge corruption.

6. **The Kingdom of God and Nonviolence:**

- Advocates of this perspective connect the concept of the Kingdom of God with nonviolence, asserting that Jesus' vision of a just society is one characterized by love, compassion, and the rejection of coercive power structures.

7. **Resisting the Sword:**
   - When Peter uses a sword to defend Jesus in the Garden of Gethsemane, Jesus rebukes him, saying, "Put your sword back into its place" (Matthew 26:52). Christian anarchists view this as a clear rejection of violence in the pursuit of justice.

8. **Nonviolent Resistance to Injustice:**
   - Christian anarchists contend that nonviolent resistance to injustice is both ethically sound and in line with Jesus' teachings. They argue that love and nonviolence are more powerful tools for social change than coercion and force.

9. **Imitating Christ's Sacrificial Love:**
   - Emphasizing the sacrificial love demonstrated by Jesus on the cross, Christian

anarchists argue that this love should be the guiding principle for confronting injustice. They see a commitment to nonviolence as an imitation of Christ's ultimate act of love.

10. **Forgiveness Over Retribution:**
   - Christian anarchists advocate for forgiveness over retribution, aligning with Jesus' teachings on forgiveness and reconciliation. They argue that a nonviolent response to wrongdoing is consistent with Christ's call for mercy and grace.

In summary, Christian anarchists draw extensively from Jesus' teachings, particularly those emphasizing love, nonviolence, and the rejection of coercive measures. They see nonviolent resistance as a powerful expression of these principles and a means to address injustice in alignment with the teachings of Christ.

13

Pointing to Jesus' rejection of earthly kingdoms during his temptation, Christian anarchists argue against the establishment of hierarchical political structures that diverge from the Kingdom of God. Here's an exploration of this perspective:

1. **The Temptation in the Wilderness:**
   - Christian anarchists refer to the account of Jesus' temptation in the wilderness (Matthew 4:8-10; Luke 4:5-8), where Satan offers him all the kingdoms of the world. Jesus responds by affirming the worship of God alone, rejecting the idea of acquiring earthly power.

2. **Rejecting Worldly Power and Authority:**
   - Jesus' refusal to succumb to the allure of earthly power becomes a foundational principle for Christian anarchists. They argue that Jesus' rejection signifies a refusal to align himself with the hierarchical political structures prevalent in the world.

3. **Kingdom of God vs. Earthly Kingdoms:**
   - Christian anarchists assert that Jesus' rejection of earthly kingdoms underscores a

fundamental distinction between the Kingdom of God and the hierarchical structures of human political systems. They argue that these earthly structures often prioritize power, control, and coercion.

4. **Jesus as a Servant King:**
   - Christian anarchists draw attention to Jesus' identity as a servant king, contrasting it with the typical model of rulership seen in earthly kingdoms. They argue that Jesus' example of servant leadership is incompatible with hierarchical political structures that rely on domination.

5. **Theological Rejection of Human Authority:**
   - This perspective is rooted in a theological rejection of human authority as the ultimate source of power. Christian anarchists contend that establishing hierarchical political structures contradicts the acknowledgment of God's sovereignty and just authority.

6. **Distinction Between God's Rule and Human Rule:**

- Christian anarchists argue that Jesus' response to the temptation highlights a crucial distinction between the rule of God and the rule of humans. They contend that earthly kingdoms often operate with self-interest and coercion, deviating from the principles of God's Kingdom.

7. **Call for a Different Model of Governance:**
   - Jesus' rejection of earthly kingdoms becomes a call for a different model of governance—one that aligns with the principles of the Kingdom of God. Christian anarchists advocate for decentralized, cooperative, and non-hierarchical structures that prioritize justice and love.

8. **Pursuit of Justice and Equity:**
   - Christian anarchists emphasize that Jesus' rejection of earthly kingdoms aligns with a broader call for justice and equity. They argue that hierarchical political structures often perpetuate injustice, and alternatives should be sought to establish a more just society.

9. **Rejecting the Temptation of Power:**
   - Christian anarchists view Jesus' resistance to the temptation of worldly power as a rejection of the corrupting influence associated with hierarchical authority. They assert that power, when centralized, can lead to oppression and moral compromise.

10. **Seeking God's Kingdom on Earth:**
   - In line with Jesus' teachings, Christian anarchists envision a society where individuals actively seek the establishment of God's Kingdom on Earth. This involves rejecting hierarchical political structures and working towards a more just, cooperative, and loving community.

In summary, Christian anarchists point to Jesus' rejection of earthly kingdoms as a pivotal moment that underscores their argument against the establishment of hierarchical political structures. They advocate for alternative models that align with the principles of the Kingdom of God—

decentralized, just, and rooted in the values of love and non-coercion.

14

Christian anarchists often reference Jesus' command to "put your sword back into its place," interpreting it as a symbolic rejection of violent means to achieve societal goals. This moment, occurring in the Garden of Gethsemane, holds significance in shaping the Christian anarchist perspective on nonviolence and resistance. Here's an exploration of this viewpoint:

1. **Context of the Garden of Gethsemane:**
   - The reference comes from the events leading up to Jesus' arrest, as described in the Gospels (Matthew 26:52; Mark 14:47; Luke 22:49-51; John 18:10-11). When a disciple (identified as Peter in some accounts) uses a sword to defend Jesus, he is commanded to put the sword back into its sheath.

2. **Symbolic Rejection of Violence:**

- Christian anarchists interpret Jesus' command as a symbolic rejection of violence as a means to achieve societal goals. They argue that the act of putting the sword away signifies a deliberate choice against using force, even in the face of imminent harm.

3. **Emphasis on Nonviolent Resistance:**
   - The incident in the Garden of Gethsemane serves as a key moment for Christian anarchists to emphasize the importance of nonviolent resistance to injustice. They argue that Jesus, facing his own arrest and persecution, exemplified a commitment to peaceful means even in the midst of turmoil.

4. **Conflict Between Kingdoms:**
   - Christian anarchists draw attention to the underlying conflict between the Kingdom of God and earthly kingdoms. By refusing to employ violence, Jesus demonstrates a commitment to a different, non-coercive approach to societal transformation—one rooted in love, justice, and the principles of God's Kingdom.

5. **Preventing the Cycle of Violence:**
   - Christian anarchists see Jesus' command as a proactive measure to prevent the escalation of violence. By restraining the use of force, they argue that Jesus aims to break the cycle of violence and present an alternative path towards justice and transformation.

6. **Alignment with Sermon on the Mount:**
   - This moment aligns with Jesus' broader teachings in the Sermon on the Mount, where he advocates for nonresistance, turning the other cheek, and loving one's enemies. Christian anarchists argue that Jesus consistently promoted a nonviolent approach to conflict.

7. **Resisting the Temptation of Force:**
   - By refusing to allow the use of force in his defense, Christian anarchists contend that Jesus resists the temptation to employ worldly means to establish God's Kingdom. They see this as a model for Christians to

resist the allure of violent methods in pursuing societal change.

8. **Demonstrating Trust in God's Plan:**
   - Christian anarchists interpret Jesus' actions as a demonstration of trust in God's plan. By forgoing violence, Jesus shows confidence that God's purposes will be fulfilled without resorting to human methods of coercion and aggression.

9. **Setting an Example for Followers:**
   - Christian anarchists view Jesus' command as setting an example for his followers. They argue that this moment serves as a foundational principle for Christians, guiding them toward a commitment to nonviolence in their own lives and interactions.

10. **A Call to Embrace the Cross:**
    - By willingly facing arrest, trial, and crucifixion without resorting to violence, Christian anarchists see Jesus' command in the Garden of Gethsemane as a call for followers to embrace the cross—the symbol of sacrificial love and redemption.

In summary, Christian anarchists reference Jesus' command to put the sword back into its place as a symbolic rejection of violent means to achieve societal goals. This moment is pivotal in shaping their commitment to nonviolent resistance, drawing inspiration from Jesus' example in the face of conflict and injustice.

15

Advocates of Christian anarchism propose decentralized, voluntary models of governance that prioritize cooperation and consensus-building over hierarchical structures. This perspective stems from a synthesis of Christian principles, particularly emphasizing the teachings of Jesus, with anarchist ideals. Here's an exploration of this viewpoint:

1. **Rejection of Coercion and Authority:**
   - Christian anarchists argue against the imposition of external authority and coercion, drawing from the belief that the ultimate

authority is God. They propose voluntary governance models that respect individual autonomy and reject hierarchical structures that may infringe on personal freedom.

2. **Biblical Foundations:**
   - Advocates find support for decentralized governance in biblical passages highlighting principles of voluntary association, cooperation, and communal living. Examples include the early Christian community described in Acts 2:44-47, where believers voluntarily shared resources.

3. **Emphasis on Jesus' Servant Leadership:**
   - Christian anarchists draw inspiration from Jesus' model of servant leadership. They argue that governance should reflect this humble and cooperative approach rather than relying on hierarchical structures that can foster inequality and exploitation.

4. **Community-Based Decision Making:**
   - The proposed models prioritize community-based decision-making processes

where individuals come together voluntarily to discuss and decide on matters affecting the community. This is seen as a manifestation of the communal spirit emphasized in Jesus' teachings.

5. **Consensus-Building Over Majority Rule:**
   - Christian anarchists favor consensus-building over majority rule in decision-making. They believe that this approach respects the dignity and opinions of every individual within the community, avoiding the potential for the oppression of minority voices.

6. **Mutual Aid and Solidarity:**
   - Anarchist Christians emphasize the biblical principles of mutual aid and solidarity. They propose governance models where individuals willingly support each other, fostering a sense of community and shared responsibility for the well-being of all.

7. **Rejecting State Authority:**

- Christian anarchists reject the authority of the state, viewing it as antithetical to the teachings of Jesus. They propose decentralized governance structures as alternatives to state authority, emphasizing self-governance at the local level.

8. **Voluntary Cooperation in Economic Systems:**
   - In economic matters, advocates of Christian anarchism propose voluntary cooperation over coercive economic systems. They envision decentralized economic models where communities voluntarily participate in fair and just economic practices.

9. **Egalitarian Principles:**
   - The decentralized governance models proposed by Christian anarchists often align with egalitarian principles. They seek to minimize hierarchical power structures, promoting equality and shared responsibility within the community.

10. **Peaceful Resolution of Conflicts:**

- Christian anarchists advocate for nonviolent and peaceful methods of conflict resolution within communities. By emphasizing consensus-building and cooperation, they aim to address disputes without resorting to hierarchical authority or coercive measures.

In summary, advocates of Christian anarchism propose decentralized, voluntary models of governance that prioritize cooperation, consensus-building, and mutual aid over hierarchical structures. This perspective seeks to align governance with Christian principles, emphasizing love, humility, and the rejection of coercive authority in building communities based on shared values and voluntary association.

16

Inspired by Jesus' teachings on community and service, Christian anarchists advocate for community-based decision-making processes that foster shared responsibility and mutual aid. This perspective draws directly from the principles articulated by Jesus in the Gospels, emphasizing humility, love, and a commitment to others. Here's an exploration of this viewpoint:

1. **The Call to Service and Humility:**
   - Christian anarchists find inspiration in Jesus' call to service and humility, as exemplified in passages such as the washing of the disciples' feet (John 13:1-17). They advocate for decision-making processes that reflect these values, prioritizing the needs of others over personal gain.

2. **Community as the Foundation:**
   - Jesus' teachings often highlight the importance of community. Christian anarchists argue that decisions impacting the community should involve all members, fostering a sense of shared responsibility and collective well-being.

3. **Equality Among Believers:**
   - The belief in the equality of all believers is central to Christian anarchist principles. Advocates assert that decision-making

processes should reflect this equality, providing each member with an equal voice and acknowledging the inherent worth of every individual.

4. **Modeling the Early Christian Community:**
   - Christian anarchists often point to the early Christian community described in Acts 2:44-47 as a model for decision-making. In this community, believers shared resources, made decisions collectively, and demonstrated mutual care for one another.

5. **Voluntary Cooperation:**
   - Emphasizing the voluntary nature of cooperation, Christian anarchists propose decision-making processes that rely on the free and willing participation of individuals. They reject coercion and advocate for consensus-building as a way to achieve unity of purpose.

6. **Non-Hierarchical Structures:**
   - In contrast to hierarchical structures, Christian anarchists favor non-hierarchical

decision-making. They argue that decisions should emerge organically from the community, reflecting the diverse perspectives and needs of its members rather than being imposed by a select few.

7. **Mutual Aid and Solidarity:**
   - Christian anarchists draw from Jesus' teachings on loving one's neighbor and the Good Samaritan parable to advocate for mutual aid and solidarity. They propose decision-making processes that prioritize the welfare of others, with a commitment to supporting those in need.

8. **Consensus-Building and Conflict Resolution:**
   - Advocates stress the importance of consensus-building in decision-making, aiming to achieve agreements that reflect the collective will of the community. They also emphasize peaceful conflict resolution methods, aligning with Jesus' teachings on reconciliation.

9. **Stewardship and Responsibility:**

- Jesus' parables, such as the Parable of the Talents (Matthew 25:14-30), inspire Christian anarchists to promote shared responsibility and stewardship within the community. Decision-making processes should reflect a commitment to collectively managing resources for the common good.

10. **Rejecting Authoritarianism:**
    - Christian anarchists reject authoritarian decision-making, asserting that the community is not to be governed by an authoritative figure or hierarchy. They propose a model where decisions arise from communal discussions, reflecting a shared commitment to service and love.

In summary, inspired by Jesus' teachings on community and service, Christian anarchists advocate for community-based decision-making processes characterized by shared responsibility, voluntary cooperation, and a commitment to mutual aid. This perspective seeks to embody the principles of love, humility, and equality found in the teachings of Jesus within the context of community governance.

17

Christian anarchists argue that justice can only be achieved through love and compassion, rejecting punitive measures and asserting that a society based on these principles aligns with Christian values. This perspective draws heavily from Jesus' teachings, particularly his emphasis on love, forgiveness, and the transformation of individuals. Here's an exploration of this viewpoint:

1. **Love as the Foundation of Christian Ethics:**
   - Christian anarchists contend that love, as emphasized by Jesus, serves as the foundational ethic for Christian living. They argue that justice, when rooted in love, leads to the holistic well-being of individuals and communities.

2. **Rejecting Retributive Justice:**

- Advocates of this perspective reject retributive justice, which seeks to punish offenders as a means of retribution. They argue that punitive measures often perpetuate cycles of violence and fail to address the underlying issues that lead to wrongdoing.

3. **Forgiveness and Reconciliation:**
   - Inspired by Jesus' teachings on forgiveness and reconciliation, Christian anarchists promote these values as central to achieving justice. They argue that genuine justice involves restoring relationships and facilitating the transformation of individuals rather than inflicting harm in return.

4. **Transformation over Retaliation:**
   - Christian anarchists emphasize the transformative power of love and compassion. They argue that justice, when approached through these principles, aims at the rehabilitation and redemption of individuals rather than seeking vengeance or perpetuating suffering.

5. **The Good Samaritan Ethic:**

  - The Good Samaritan parable serves as a foundational illustration for Christian anarchists. They highlight the Samaritan's compassionate response to the wounded man as a model for how society should approach issues of injustice—with a focus on caring for those in need.

6. **Jesus' Challenge to the Pharisees:**
   - In encounters with the Pharisees, Jesus challenged their legalistic approach to justice. Christian anarchists draw from these interactions to argue against a rigid, punitive understanding of justice and advocate for a more compassionate and merciful approach.

7. **Society Reflecting Christian Values:**
   - Christian anarchists envision a society that reflects Christian values of love and compassion in its justice system. They argue for structures that prioritize rehabilitation, restoration, and community support over punishment and isolation.

8. **Redemption and Second Chances:**

- Rooted in the belief in redemption, Christian anarchists advocate for a justice system that provides individuals with second chances. They emphasize the possibility of transformation and the restoration of dignity for those who have committed wrongs.

9. **Caring for the Marginalized:**
   - Christian anarchists argue that a just society based on love and compassion actively cares for the marginalized and vulnerable. This involves addressing root causes of injustice, such as poverty and systemic inequality, rather than solely focusing on punitive measures.

10. **Promoting Healing and Wholeness:**
   - Christian anarchists see justice as a means of promoting healing and wholeness, both for victims and offenders. They contend that a society built on love and compassion actively works toward restoring individuals to a state of well-being and integration into the community.

In summary, Christian anarchists argue that justice, as understood through the lens of love and compassion, aligns with Christian values. They reject punitive measures in favor of a justice system focused on transformation, restoration, and the holistic well-being of individuals and communities. This perspective seeks to embody the teachings of Jesus in creating a more compassionate and just society.

18

The Sermon on the Mount serves as a blueprint for Christian anarchists, guiding them to embody humility, peacemaking, and love for enemies in their interactions and societal structures. This foundational text from the Gospel of Matthew (chapters 5-7) contains some of Jesus' most profound teachings, which resonate deeply with the principles advocated by Christian anarchists. Here's an exploration of how the Sermon on the Mount influences their perspective:

1. **Emphasis on Humility:**

- Jesus begins the Sermon on the Mount with the Beatitudes, which highlight the virtues of humility, meekness, and poverty of spirit. Christian anarchists see humility as essential for dismantling oppressive power structures and promoting equality within society.

2. **Peacemaking and Reconciliation:**
   - Jesus' teachings on peacemaking are central to the Sermon on the Mount. Christian anarchists interpret this as a call to actively pursue peace and reconciliation in all aspects of life, both personally and within societal structures. They advocate for nonviolent conflict resolution and the dismantling of systems that perpetuate violence and oppression.

3. **Love for Enemies:**
   - One of the most challenging teachings of Jesus in the Sermon on the Mount is his command to love one's enemies and pray for those who persecute you. Christian anarchists see this as a radical call to break the cycle of violence and hatred, advocating for

forgiveness, reconciliation, and the transformation of relationships.

4. **Non-Retaliation and Nonviolence:**
   - Jesus instructs his followers not to retaliate against those who wrong them but to turn the other cheek and go the extra mile. Christian anarchists interpret this as a rejection of violence and a commitment to nonviolent resistance in the face of oppression. They see nonviolence as a powerful tool for social change and justice.

5. **Critique of Religious Hypocrisy:**
   - Throughout the Sermon on the Mount, Jesus critiques religious hypocrisy and calls his followers to live with integrity and authenticity. Christian anarchists apply this critique to societal structures, advocating for transparency, accountability, and a rejection of systems that perpetuate injustice under the guise of religion or morality.

6. **The Lord's Prayer:**
   - In the Lord's Prayer, Jesus teaches his disciples to pray for God's kingdom to come

and his will to be done on earth as it is in heaven. Christian anarchists see this as a call to actively work towards the establishment of God's kingdom—a society characterized by justice, love, and peace—here and now.

7. **Seeking First the Kingdom of God:**
   - Jesus concludes the Sermon on the Mount by urging his followers to seek first the kingdom of God and his righteousness. Christian anarchists interpret this as a prioritization of God's values over worldly concerns, advocating for a society that aligns with the principles of God's kingdom rather than the values of empire or earthly powers.

8. **Living Counter-Culturally:**
   - The teachings of the Sermon on the Mount often run counter to the values and priorities of mainstream society. Christian anarchists see themselves as called to live counter-culturally, challenging the status quo and embodying an alternative way of life based on the teachings of Jesus.

9. **Building Community and Solidarity:**

- The Sermon on the Mount emphasizes the importance of community, prayer, and mutual support among believers. Christian anarchists see this as a model for building communities of solidarity and care that extend beyond traditional boundaries of nationality, ethnicity, or social status.

10. **A Vision for a Just and Peaceful Society:**
    - Overall, the Sermon on the Mount provides Christian anarchists with a vision for a just and peaceful society—a society characterized by humility, peacemaking, love for enemies, and a commitment to God's kingdom values. They see this vision as not only aspirational but also attainable through the transformative power of God's grace and the active participation of believers in shaping societal structures.

In summary, the Sermon on the Mount serves as a guiding framework for Christian anarchists, shaping their values, priorities, and vision for society. It calls them to embody humility, peacemaking, and love for enemies in their interactions and societal structures, reflecting the transformative and radical message of Jesus.

19

The ultimate goal for Christian anarchists is to work towards the establishment of a "Kingdom of God on Earth," characterized by love, justice, and nonviolence, aligning their vision with the teachings of Jesus. This aspiration reflects a deeply theological and ethical commitment to embodying the values espoused by Jesus in the Gospels and to creating a society that mirrors the principles of God's kingdom. Here's an exploration of this overarching goal:

1. **Biblical Foundation:**
   - Christian anarchists derive their ultimate goal from the biblical narrative, especially Jesus' teachings about the Kingdom of God. They draw from passages such as the Lord's Prayer (Matthew 6:10), where believers are instructed to pray for God's kingdom to come on earth as it is in heaven.

2. **Kingdom Values:**
   - The Kingdom of God, as envisioned by Christian anarchists, is characterized by values such as love, justice, mercy, humility, and nonviolence. They see these principles as the core of Jesus' teachings and strive to implement them in their personal lives and advocate for them in societal structures.

3. **Rejecting Earthly Systems of Power:**
   - Christian anarchists reject reliance on earthly systems of power and authority, believing that these often lead to oppression, exploitation, and violence. Instead, they seek to establish a society where God's principles govern, and individuals willingly follow the path of love, justice, and peace.

4. **Nonviolent Social Transformation:**
   - Central to the Christian anarchist vision is the concept of nonviolent social transformation. They reject the use of force or coercion in achieving their goals, taking inspiration from Jesus' nonviolent approach to addressing social and political issues.

5. **Imitating Christ's Model:**
   - Christian anarchists aim to imitate Christ's model of leadership and love. They believe that by embodying the qualities exemplified by Jesus—such as humility, self-sacrifice, and compassion—they contribute to the establishment of a society that reflects the values of the Kingdom of God.

6. **Active Participation in Social Justice:**
   - The pursuit of the Kingdom of God on Earth involves active participation in social justice. Christian anarchists engage in efforts to address systemic injustices, alleviate suffering, and promote equality, guided by their understanding of Jesus' call to love and serve others.

7. **Building Communities of Solidarity:**
   - Christian anarchists envision communities of solidarity where individuals actively support and care for one another. These communities, they believe, are the building blocks of the Kingdom of God on Earth,

reflecting a shared commitment to justice, equality, and mutual aid.

8. **Rejecting Earthly Hierarchies:**
   - The vision for the Kingdom of God on Earth includes a rejection of earthly hierarchies and power structures. Christian anarchists advocate for non-hierarchical, cooperative models of governance that prioritize the well-being of all individuals within the community.

9. **Spiritual and Social Transformation:**
   - Christian anarchists see the establishment of the Kingdom of God on Earth as both a spiritual and social transformation. It involves individuals embracing the teachings of Jesus in their personal lives and actively working towards reshaping societal structures to align with these principles.

10. **Hope for a Just and Peaceful World:**
   - Ultimately, the goal of Christian anarchists is to contribute to the realization of a just and peaceful world. They believe that by embodying the teachings of Jesus and

actively working towards the establishment of the Kingdom of God on Earth, they can contribute to the flourishing of a society characterized by love, justice, and nonviolence.

In summary, the ultimate goal for Christian anarchists is to work towards the establishment of a Kingdom of God on Earth—a society characterized by love, justice, and nonviolence. This vision is deeply rooted in their understanding of Jesus' teachings and represents a commitment to both personal and societal transformation guided by the principles of God's kingdom.

20

Drawing from Jesus' critiques of religious authorities in his time, Christian anarchists argue against hierarchical religious structures. They contend that Jesus' emphasis on humility and service challenges institutionalized religious power, supporting an anarchist perspective. Here's an exploration of this viewpoint:

1. **Jesus' Challenge to Religious Hypocrisy:**
   - Christian anarchists point to instances in the Gospels where Jesus strongly criticizes religious leaders, particularly the Pharisees and scribes, for their hypocrisy and self-righteousness. They argue that Jesus' critiques serve as a foundation for questioning hierarchical religious structures that prioritize external appearances over genuine humility and service.

2. **Emphasis on Servant Leadership:**
   - Jesus consistently teaches the value of servant leadership throughout his ministry. Christian anarchists draw from passages like Mark 10:42-45, where Jesus emphasizes that true greatness comes from serving others. They argue that hierarchical religious structures often contradict this principle by promoting positions of authority and power.

3. **Dismantling Power Dynamics:**
   - Christian anarchists see Jesus' critiques as a call to dismantle power dynamics within

religious institutions. They contend that hierarchical structures tend to concentrate authority in a few individuals, fostering a system that is antithetical to the humble and servant-oriented leadership advocated by Jesus.

4. **Equality Among Believers:**
   - The teachings of Jesus emphasize the equality of believers in the eyes of God. Christian anarchists argue that hierarchical religious structures undermine this equality by creating distinctions between clergy and laity. They advocate for a model that fosters a sense of shared responsibility and mutual respect among all believers.

5. **Jesus' Model of Humility:**
   - Jesus' own life exemplifies humility and service. Christian anarchists assert that hierarchical religious structures, with their centralized authority, often deviate from this model. They advocate for a decentralized approach that promotes the humility demonstrated by Jesus in his interactions with others.

6. **Challenging Authoritarianism in Religion:**
   - Christian anarchists challenge the authoritarian tendencies present in certain religious structures. They argue that Jesus' confrontations with religious authorities serve as a model for resisting oppressive systems that prioritize control and conformity over genuine spiritual growth and compassion.

7. **Community-Centered Spirituality:**
   - Anarchist Christians envision a community-centered spirituality, where believers come together as equals to share in the responsibilities and joys of their faith. They argue that hierarchical religious structures can hinder the development of genuine community by creating barriers between clergy and the rest of the congregation.

8. **Empowering Every Believer:**
   - Jesus' teachings empower every believer to serve and contribute to the well-being of the community. Christian anarchists contend

that hierarchical structures disempower the majority of believers by limiting their active involvement in decision-making and ministry. They advocate for models that empower and encourage the diverse gifts within the community.

9. **Critique of Religious Elitism:**
   - Jesus' critiques challenge the elitism present in religious structures of his time. Christian anarchists extend this critique to contemporary hierarchical systems, arguing that they can perpetuate an exclusive and elitist approach to spirituality, contrary to the inclusive message of Jesus.

10. **Reclaiming the Early Christian Egalitarian Spirit:**
   - Christian anarchists look to the early Christian communities described in the New Testament, where believers shared resources and responsibilities without a rigid hierarchy. They argue that reclaiming this egalitarian spirit is not only consistent with Jesus' teachings but also essential for fostering genuine Christian community.

In summary, drawing from Jesus' critiques of religious authorities, Christian anarchists argue against hierarchical religious structures. They contend that Jesus' emphasis on humility, service, and equality challenges institutionalized religious power and supports an anarchist perspective that values decentralization, community, and the empowerment of every believer.

21

Christian anarchists point to the egalitarian nature of early Christian communities, as described in Acts 2:44-47. This biblical example serves as a precedent for voluntary cooperation, mutual aid, and a rejection of hierarchical structures. Here's an exploration of this perspective:

1. **Biblical Foundation in Acts 2:44-47:**
   - Christian anarchists draw from the account of the early Christian community in Acts 2:44-47, which describes believers sharing everything they had, living in unity,

and supporting one another. This serves as a foundational example for Christian anarchists advocating for communal living and rejecting hierarchical structures.

2. **Voluntary Cooperation and Sharing:**
   - The early Christians voluntarily cooperated in sharing their possessions and resources. Christian anarchists argue that this voluntary sharing reflects the principles of mutual aid and cooperation, as opposed to coerced redistribution or top-down management.

3. **Rejection of Private Property:**
   - Acts 2:44-47 highlights the communal aspect of early Christian life, with believers selling their possessions and having all things in common. Christian anarchists use this as a precedent for rejecting the concept of private property, advocating for a communal approach where resources are shared for the common good.

4. **Equality Among Believers:**

- The egalitarian nature of the early Christian community challenges hierarchical structures. Christian anarchists assert that this equality among believers, irrespective of their socio-economic status, ethnicity, or background, should be a guiding principle in contemporary Christian communities.

5. **Mutual Aid and Support:**
   - The Acts passage demonstrates a commitment to mutual aid and support within the Christian community. Christian anarchists argue that this model encourages active care for one another, fostering a sense of solidarity and interconnectedness that opposes hierarchical structures that may foster inequality.

6. **Community-Based Decision Making:**
   - The communal decision-making process in Acts, where believers made decisions together, is seen by Christian anarchists as a rejection of centralized authority. They advocate for community-based decision-making processes that involve the active

participation of all members rather than decisions imposed from above.

7. **Dismantling Economic Disparities:**
   - Christian anarchists point to the economic equality in the early Christian community as a model for dismantling economic disparities. They contend that hierarchical structures can perpetuate economic inequality, whereas voluntary cooperation and shared resources promote economic justice.

8. **Living Counter-Culturally:**
   - Christian anarchists see the early Christian community as living counter-culturally in the context of the Roman Empire. Similarly, they aim to live counter-culturally in contemporary society by rejecting hierarchical norms and embracing a more communal and egalitarian way of life.

9. **Critique of Institutionalized Religion:**
   - Acts 2:44-47 provides a counterpoint to institutionalized religion. Christian anarchists argue that the early Christians embodied a more authentic and grassroots expression of

faith, one that rejected rigid religious structures in favor of a community-centered, egalitarian spirituality.

10. **Model for Christian Anarchist Communities:**
   - The early Christian community in Acts serves as a model for contemporary Christian anarchist communities. Christian anarchists seek to establish communities that reflect the voluntary cooperation, mutual aid, and rejection of hierarchical structures found in this biblical example.

In summary, Christian anarchists point to the egalitarian nature of early Christian communities, specifically described in Acts 2:44-47. This biblical example serves as a precedent for voluntary cooperation, mutual aid, and a rejection of hierarchical structures, influencing the principles and practices advocated by Christian anarchists in their pursuit of a more just and equitable society.

22

Advocates of Christian anarchism reject the elevation of national interests above the commandment to love one's neighbor. They argue that the Kingdom of God transcends national boundaries, promoting a global community based on love, justice, and solidarity. Here's an exploration of this perspective:

1. **Primacy of the Commandment to Love:**
   - Christian anarchists prioritize Jesus' commandment to love one's neighbor as a foundational principle. They argue that this commandment takes precedence over national interests and requires a commitment to fostering love, justice, and solidarity on a global scale.

2. **Critique of Nationalism:**
   - Christian anarchists critique nationalism as an ideology that can lead to the prioritization of one's own nation at the expense of others. They assert that elevating national interests above the commandment to love one's neighbor can contribute to

division, conflict, and the neglect of the global community.

3. **Jesus' Inclusive Definition of Neighbor:**
   - Christian anarchists emphasize Jesus' inclusive definition of neighbor, as demonstrated in the Parable of the Good Samaritan (Luke 10:25-37). They argue that this parable challenges narrow, nationalistic perspectives by highlighting the universal call to extend love and compassion beyond cultural and national boundaries.

4. **Global Scope of God's Kingdom:**
   - Advocates of Christian anarchism assert that the Kingdom of God, as envisioned by Jesus, transcends national borders. They contend that God's kingdom is a global community characterized by love, justice, and solidarity, inviting believers to prioritize these values over nationalistic agendas.

5. **Rejecting Divisive Us vs. Them Mentalities:**

- Christian anarchists reject divisive "us vs. them" mentalities that can arise from excessive nationalism. They argue that such mentalities undermine the Christian call to embrace all people as neighbors, fostering a sense of shared humanity that extends beyond geopolitical boundaries.

6. **Global Implications of Christian Ethics:**
   - Christian anarchists believe that Christian ethics, rooted in the teachings of Jesus, have global implications. They assert that principles like love, forgiveness, and justice should guide interactions not only within national borders but also in relationships with people from different nations and cultures.

7. **Solidarity with the Marginalized Worldwide:**
   - Christian anarchists advocate for solidarity with the marginalized and oppressed on a global scale. They argue that focusing solely on national interests may contribute to the perpetuation of global inequalities, whereas a commitment to love

and justice requires addressing the needs of the vulnerable worldwide.

8. **Promoting International Cooperation:**
   - In rejecting the elevation of national interests, Christian anarchists support international cooperation and collaboration. They believe that global challenges, such as poverty, environmental issues, and social injustice, necessitate collaborative efforts that prioritize the well-being of all people, regardless of their nationality.

9. **Pacifist Stance Against Nationalistic Conflicts:**
   - Christian anarchists, often adopting pacifist stances, reject nationalistic conflicts that lead to violence and warfare. They argue that such conflicts contradict the principles of love and solidarity promoted by Jesus, advocating for peaceful resolutions that prioritize the common good of all humanity.

10. **Global Community Reflecting Kingdom Values:**

- Ultimately, advocates of Christian anarchism envision a global community that reflects the values of the Kingdom of God—love, justice, and solidarity. They argue for a worldview that transcends national boundaries, fostering a sense of interconnectedness and shared responsibility for the well-being of the entire human family.

In summary, advocates of Christian anarchism reject the elevation of national interests above the commandment to love one's neighbor. They argue for a global community based on the values of the Kingdom of God, emphasizing love, justice, and solidarity across national boundaries. This perspective challenges narrow nationalism in favor of a more inclusive and compassionate worldview rooted in the teachings of Jesus.

23

Christian anarchists emphasize Paul's exhortation in Romans 12:2 to not conform to the patterns of the world. They argue that worldly systems often promote inequality and violence, advocating for nonconformity and the pursuit of alternative, just structures. Here's an exploration of this perspective:

1. **Biblical Basis in Romans 12:2:**
   - Christian anarchists draw from Paul's letter to the Romans, specifically Romans 12:2, where believers are urged not to conform to the patterns of the world but to be transformed by the renewing of their minds. This biblical foundation serves as a call for Christians to resist adopting societal structures that may perpetuate injustice and violence.

2. **Rejecting Unjust Worldly Systems:**
   - Christian anarchists interpret Paul's exhortation as a call to reject systems that perpetuate inequality, exploitation, and violence. They argue that conforming to such systems goes against the transformative message of Christ, prompting a commitment to alternative, just structures.

3. **Worldly Patterns of Exploitation:**

- Christian anarchists identify worldly patterns that exploit individuals and create hierarchical structures. They argue that conforming to such patterns, whether in economic, political, or social realms, contradicts the teachings of Jesus, who advocated for love, compassion, and justice.

4. **Inequality and Social Injustice:**
   - The conforming to worldly patterns often leads to systems that perpetuate inequality and social injustice. Christian anarchists contend that Paul's exhortation calls believers to resist participating in or supporting structures that contribute to the marginalization and mistreatment of certain groups within society.

5. **Nonconformity as a Call to Justice:**
   - Christian anarchists view nonconformity as a call to pursue justice and equality. They argue that conforming to unjust worldly systems can compromise the Christian commitment to love and serve others, prompting the need for alternative structures

aligned with the principles of the Kingdom of God.

6. **Transformative Renewal of the Mind:**
   - The renewal of the mind, as mentioned in Romans 12:2, is seen by Christian anarchists as a transformative process guided by Christian principles. This renewal prompts believers to question and challenge societal norms that contradict the values of love, compassion, and justice.

7. **Promoting Peaceful Alternatives:**
   - Christian anarchists advocate for nonviolent alternatives to worldly systems that often rely on coercion and force. They argue that conforming to patterns of violence contradicts the teachings of Jesus, promoting a commitment to peaceful resolutions and just structures.

8. **Counter-Cultural Witness:**
   - Nonconformity to worldly patterns becomes a counter-cultural witness for Christian anarchists. They believe that living in a manner distinct from the prevailing

norms challenges the status quo and serves as a testimony to the transformative power of Christian values.

9. **Modeling Kingdom Values:**
   - Christian anarchists see nonconformity as an opportunity to model the values of the Kingdom of God. They argue that conforming to worldly patterns diminishes the distinctive witness Christians can have in society, while actively pursuing just alternatives aligns with the teachings of Jesus.

10. **Participating in God's Renewal:**
   - By actively resisting conformity to unjust patterns, Christian anarchists participate in God's renewal of the world. They argue that this renewal involves creating structures that reflect divine values of love, justice, and equality, embodying a vision for a society transformed by the principles of the Kingdom.

In summary, Christian anarchists emphasize Paul's exhortation in Romans 12:2 to not conform to the patterns of the world. They argue that this call prompts believers to resist participating in unjust and violent systems, advocating for nonconformity and the pursuit of alternative, just structures rooted in the transformative message of Christ.

24

Christian anarchists draw from biblical passages critiquing the establishment of earthly kingdoms, such as 1 Samuel 8, where God warns against the consequences of human kingship. They contend that this critique supports their rejection of centralized political authority. Here's an exploration of this perspective:

1. **1 Samuel 8 as a Warning Against Human Kingship:**
   - Christian anarchists point to 1 Samuel 8 in the Old Testament, where the Israelites demand a king to rule over them. God warns through the prophet Samuel about the negative consequences of human kingship, including conscription, taxation, and loss of personal freedoms. This biblical narrative

serves as a cautionary tale against the centralization of political power.

2. **God as the Ultimate Authority:**
   - Christian anarchists emphasize the overarching theme in the Bible that God is the ultimate authority. They argue that placing trust in human rulers and establishing centralized political authority undermines the divine sovereignty and leads to systems that may not align with God's principles of justice and love.

3. **Human Kingship vs. God's Rule:**
   - Drawing from 1 Samuel 8, Christian anarchists contrast human kingship with the idea of God's direct rule. They contend that the desire for centralized political authority reflects a lack of faith in God's ability to guide and govern the people directly without the need for human rulers.

4. **Dangers of Concentrated Power:**
   - Christian anarchists highlight the dangers associated with concentrated political power, as outlined in 1 Samuel 8. They argue that

centralized authority often leads to oppression, injustice, and the prioritization of the ruler's interests over the well-being of the community.

5. **Rejection of Earthly Hierarchies:**
   - The critique of human kingship in 1 Samuel 8 supports Christian anarchists' rejection of earthly hierarchies. They argue that the establishment of kingship introduces hierarchical structures that can lead to exploitation and a departure from the principles of equality and justice advocated by God.

6. **Jesus as the True King:**
   - Christian anarchists see Jesus as the true King, contrasting the model of kingship presented in 1 Samuel 8. They argue that Jesus' reign is characterized by servant leadership, humility, and a commitment to the well-being of all people, providing an alternative to the oppressive nature of human kingship.

7. **Seeking God's Guidance Over Human Rulership:**
   - Christian anarchists advocate for seeking God's guidance over relying on human rulership. They contend that 1 Samuel 8 encourages believers to prioritize divine wisdom and discernment rather than placing trust in centralized political authority that may deviate from God's intended order.

8. **Theocracy vs. Human Governance:**
   - The critique in 1 Samuel 8 raises questions about theocracy versus human governance. Christian anarchists argue that while theocracy involves direct divine rule, human governance often introduces flawed systems that can lead to corruption and the abuse of power.

9. **Anarchist Principles in the Bible:**
   - Christian anarchists find support for their rejection of centralized political authority within the broader context of biblical themes promoting justice, equality, and freedom. They argue that these principles align more

closely with an anarchist worldview than with systems of human kingship.

10. **Advocating for Decentralized Governance:**
   - In light of 1 Samuel 8, Christian anarchists advocate for decentralized forms of governance. They believe that a rejection of centralized political authority aligns with the biblical narrative and promotes systems that reflect God's values of justice, compassion, and collective well-being.

In summary, Christian anarchists draw from biblical passages like 1 Samuel 8, critiquing the establishment of earthly kingdoms and central political authority. They contend that this critique supports their rejection of centralized governance, emphasizing the need for divine guidance and decentralized systems that align with biblical principles of justice and equality.

Christian anarchists highlight the early church's anti-imperialist stance against the Roman Empire. They argue that this historical context reinforces the Christian call to resist oppressive powers and aligns with anarchist principles of opposing coercive authority. Here's an exploration of this perspective:

1. **Context of Imperial Oppression:**
   - Christian anarchists draw attention to the historical context in which the early Christian communities emerged—the Roman Empire, known for its imperialistic and coercive rule. They argue that the early Christians faced systemic oppression and exploitation under Roman authority.

2. **Imperialism and Injustice:**
   - Christian anarchists contend that the Roman Empire embodied imperialistic values that often led to social injustice, exploitation, and the consolidation of power in the hands of a few. They assert that the early Christians' resistance to this imperial order aligns with

the principles of justice and equality advocated by Jesus.

3. **Early Christian Nonconformity:**
   - Christian anarchists highlight the nonconformist stance of early Christians in the face of imperial pressure to conform to Roman religious and political practices. They argue that this nonconformity reflects an early form of Christian anarchism—a rejection of coercive authority and an affirmation of alternative, just structures.

4. **Jesus as a Subversive Figure:**
   - Christian anarchists see Jesus as a subversive figure challenging the oppressive powers of his time. They argue that the early Christian resistance to the Roman Empire is an extension of Jesus' call to resist systems that perpetuate inequality, exploitation, and violence.

5. **Christian Martyrdom as Resistance:**
   - The willingness of early Christians to face persecution and martyrdom is viewed by Christian anarchists as a form of resistance

against the imperial powers. They argue that this commitment to principles of justice and faithfulness to Christ demonstrates a rejection of coercive authority in favor of a higher moral imperative.

6. **Counter-Cultural Witness:**
   - Christian anarchists see the early Christian communities as a counter-cultural witness against the imperialistic norms of the Roman Empire. They argue that the Christian commitment to love, compassion, and nonviolence provided an alternative vision that opposed the coercive and oppressive structures of the time.

7. **Pauline Letters and Resistance:**
   - Christian anarchists refer to Pauline letters, where Paul often challenged the imperial authority of Rome indirectly. They argue that Paul's teachings on justice, equality, and the inclusive nature of the Christian community aligned with anarchist principles of opposing coercive authority and promoting a more egalitarian society.

8. **Biblical Roots of Resistance:**
   - Christian anarchists root their resistance to coercive authority in biblical narratives, such as the early Christians' resistance against the Roman Empire. They argue that these stories provide a foundation for contemporary Christian anarchists to resist oppressive powers and systems.

9. **Kingdom of God vs. Imperial Rule:**
   - Christian anarchists contrast the imperial rule of the Roman Empire with the concept of the Kingdom of God preached by Jesus. They argue that the Christian call to seek the Kingdom of God is inherently anti-imperialist, emphasizing a higher allegiance to God's just and loving rule.

10. **Anarchist Principles in Christian Resistance:**
   - Christian anarchists find resonance between the early Christian resistance to the Roman Empire and modern anarchist principles. They argue that the rejection of coercive authority, the pursuit of justice, and the establishment of alternative, egalitarian

structures align with the historical Christian resistance against imperial oppression.

In summary, Christian anarchists highlight the early church's anti-imperialist stance against the Roman Empire, seeing it as a historical context that reinforces the Christian call to resist oppressive powers. They argue that this resistance aligns with anarchist principles of opposing coercive authority, promoting justice, and advocating for alternative, just structures based on the teachings of Jesus.

26

Christian anarchists stress Jesus' inclusivity and concern for the marginalized. They argue that a society based on these values requires the dismantling of hierarchical structures that perpetuate discrimination, promoting a more inclusive and equitable community. Here's an exploration of this perspective:

1. **Inclusivity in Jesus' Ministry:**

- Christian anarchists emphasize Jesus' ministry, which was characterized by inclusivity. They point to instances where Jesus welcomed and engaged with people from all walks of life, breaking societal norms of exclusivity.

2. **Radical Love for All:**
   - Jesus' command to love one another, irrespective of societal divisions, serves as a foundational principle for Christian anarchists. They argue that hierarchical structures often contribute to the exclusion of certain groups, while Jesus' radical love calls for the dismantling of such barriers.

3. **Concern for the Marginalized:**
   - Jesus consistently demonstrated a special concern for the marginalized—the poor, the sick, and those on the fringes of society. Christian anarchists assert that this concern is a call to address systemic issues that contribute to marginalization and to challenge hierarchical structures that perpetuate inequality.

4. **Challenging Social Hierarchies:**
   - Christian anarchists view Jesus' actions as a challenge to existing social hierarchies. They argue that hierarchical structures often marginalize and oppress certain groups, and Jesus' inclusive approach challenges these structures, calling for a more egalitarian society.

5. **Rejection of Exclusivity:**
   - Jesus' rejection of exclusivity is a central theme for Christian anarchists. They argue that hierarchical structures can create exclusive spaces, and Jesus' teachings call for the breakdown of these barriers, promoting a community where everyone is valued and included.

6. **Equality Before God:**
   - Christian anarchists draw on the idea of equality before God. They argue that hierarchical structures go against the Christian belief that all individuals, regardless of their social status, are equal in the eyes of God. Jesus' inclusive ministry reinforces this perspective.

7. **Dismantling Discriminatory Systems:**
   - Christian anarchists advocate for the dismantling of discriminatory systems that perpetuate inequality. They argue that Jesus' inclusive approach challenges the discriminatory practices embedded in societal structures, calling for a reevaluation of systems that perpetuate discrimination.

8. **Active Solidarity with the Marginalized:**
   - Jesus' active solidarity with the marginalized serves as a model for Christian anarchists. They contend that hierarchical structures often lead to the neglect of the marginalized, and Jesus' example calls for active engagement, advocacy, and the dismantling of systems that perpetuate injustice.

9. **Empowerment of the Vulnerable:**
   - Christian anarchists highlight Jesus' empowerment of the vulnerable, including women, children, and those considered outcasts. They argue that hierarchical

structures often disempower certain groups, and Jesus' teachings call for the upliftment and empowerment of the vulnerable in society.

10. **Formation of Inclusive Communities:**
   - Christian anarchists envision the formation of inclusive communities that reflect Jesus' values. They argue that hierarchical structures can create divisions, and Jesus' inclusivity encourages the creation of communities where diversity is celebrated, and everyone has a place.

In summary, Christian anarchists stress Jesus' inclusivity and concern for the marginalized, asserting that a society based on these values requires the dismantling of hierarchical structures that perpetuate discrimination. They advocate for a more inclusive and equitable community, guided by the principles of love, justice, and equality exemplified in the teachings and actions of Jesus.

27

Christian anarchists draw on biblical critiques of wealth accumulation, such as Jesus' warnings about the dangers of wealth in the Sermon on the Mount (Matthew 6:19-21). They advocate for economic systems that prioritize community well-being over individual prosperity. Here's an exploration of this perspective:

1. **Jesus' Warning Against Treasures on Earth:**
   - Christian anarchists refer to Jesus' explicit warnings in the Sermon on the Mount, where he cautions against accumulating treasures on earth. In Matthew 6:19-21, Jesus advises storing treasures in heaven rather than on earth, highlighting the spiritual dangers of prioritizing wealth.

2. **Focus on Eternal Values:**
   - Jesus' critique of wealth accumulation prompts Christian anarchists to focus on eternal values rather than material possessions. They argue that the pursuit of

individual prosperity can lead to a distortion of priorities and values, emphasizing the need for economic systems that align with spiritual and communal well-being.

3. **Challenging the Idolatry of Wealth:**
   - Christian anarchists see Jesus' warnings as a challenge to the idolatry of wealth. They argue that the accumulation of wealth can become a substitute for a deeper connection with God and a distraction from the communal responsibility to care for one another.

4. **Economic Justice and Equity:**
   - Christian anarchists advocate for economic systems that prioritize justice and equity. They argue that the biblical critique of wealth accumulation aligns with the call for economic structures that ensure fair distribution of resources, minimizing disparities between the affluent and the marginalized.

5. **Shared Resources and Mutual Aid:**

- The emphasis on community well-being in Christian anarchist thought leads to a promotion of shared resources and mutual aid. They argue that economic systems should be built on principles of cooperation, where individuals contribute based on their abilities, and resources are distributed based on the needs of the community.

6. **Rejecting Exploitative Capitalism:**
   - Christian anarchists critique exploitative forms of capitalism that prioritize individual wealth accumulation at the expense of others. They argue that such systems often perpetuate social inequalities and fail to uphold the communal values espoused in the teachings of Jesus.

7. **Community-Centered Economic Models:**
   - Christian anarchists envision economic models that prioritize community needs. They argue for decentralized, community-centered structures that empower local communities to make decisions about resource allocation and

economic activities, fostering a sense of shared responsibility.

8. **Stewardship and Responsible Resource Use:**
   - Drawing from biblical principles, Christian anarchists emphasize stewardship and responsible resource use. They argue that economic systems should prioritize sustainable practices and responsible management of resources, reflecting a commitment to caring for God's creation.

9. **Resisting Consumerism:**
   - Christian anarchists resist the consumerist culture that often accompanies wealth accumulation. They argue that Jesus' warnings about treasures on earth call for a rejection of excessive consumption and a shift toward a more sustainable and mindful approach to economic life.

10. **Emphasis on Generosity and Charity:**
    - Christian anarchists emphasize the importance of generosity and charity as

alternatives to wealth accumulation. They argue for economic systems that promote a culture of giving, sharing, and supporting one another, reflecting the selfless love exemplified by Jesus.

In summary, Christian anarchists draw on biblical critiques of wealth accumulation, particularly Jesus' warnings in the Sermon on the Mount, to advocate for economic systems that prioritize community well-being over individual prosperity. They emphasize the dangers of idolizing wealth, promoting economic justice, shared resources, and responsible stewardship as integral components of a more just and equitable society.

28

Christian anarchists align with the prophetic tradition in the Bible, where figures like Amos and Isaiah challenged social injustice. They argue that this tradition supports their call for dismantling oppressive structures and advocating for a more just and equitable society. Here's an exploration of this perspective:

1. **Biblical Prophetic Tradition:**
   - Christian anarchists draw inspiration from the prophetic tradition in the Bible, where figures like Amos, Isaiah, and other prophets spoke out against social injustice, exploitation, and the oppression of the vulnerable.

2. **Amos' Critique of Injustice:**
   - Amos, in the Old Testament, vehemently criticized the economic and social injustices prevailing in Israel. Christian anarchists highlight Amos' condemnation of the exploitation of the poor, corrupt practices, and the neglect of justice as a resonant call for contemporary Christians to challenge oppressive structures.

3. **Isaiah's Call for Justice:**
   - Isaiah, another prophetic figure, called for justice, righteousness, and the care of the marginalized. Christian anarchists see Isaiah's prophetic vision as a blueprint for challenging

systemic injustices and dismantling structures that perpetuate inequality.

4. **Prophetic Courage in Speaking Truth:**
   - Christian anarchists admire the prophetic courage displayed by figures like Amos and Isaiah. They argue that the prophetic tradition encourages believers to speak truth to power, challenging oppressive structures with the aim of promoting justice and equity.

5. **Confrontation of Economic Exploitation:**
   - The prophetic tradition often involved a confrontation with economic exploitation and the mistreatment of the poor. Christian anarchists align with this tradition by critiquing economic systems that prioritize the accumulation of wealth at the expense of the vulnerable.

6. **Challenge to Religious Hypocrisy:**
   - The prophets often challenged religious hypocrisy and ritualistic practices devoid of justice. Christian anarchists draw on this critique to challenge hierarchical religious

structures that may perpetuate injustice, advocating for a more authentic and justice-oriented expression of faith.

7. **Rooted in God's Concern for the Oppressed:**
   - Christian anarchists argue that the prophetic tradition is rooted in God's concern for the oppressed. They see the prophetic call as a reflection of God's desire for a just and equitable society, aligning with their own call to dismantle oppressive structures and systems.

8. **Parallel to Jesus' Activism:**
   - Christian anarchists draw parallels between the prophetic tradition and the activism of Jesus. They argue that Jesus, like the prophets, challenged oppressive systems, confronted injustice, and called for a transformation of society based on love, compassion, and justice.

9. **Dismantling Systems of Exploitation:**
   - Christian anarchists advocate for the dismantling of systems that perpetuate

exploitation and oppression. They see the prophetic tradition as a guide for challenging unjust structures, whether they be economic, political, or social, in order to create a more equitable society.

10. **Call for Social Transformation:**
   - The prophetic tradition supports Christian anarchists in their call for social transformation. They argue that, like the prophets of old, contemporary believers are called to challenge oppressive structures and work towards a society where justice and compassion prevail.

In summary, Christian anarchists align with the prophetic tradition in the Bible, particularly figures like Amos and Isaiah, who challenged social injustice. They see this tradition as a source of inspiration and guidance for their own advocacy in dismantling oppressive structures and promoting a more just and equitable society rooted in the values of love, compassion, and justice.

29

Christian anarchists argue that the biblical concept of radical equality in God's eyes challenges hierarchical structures and supports an anarchist vision of a society without coercive authority. Here's an exploration of this perspective:

1. **Biblical Foundation of Radical Equality:**
   - Christian anarchists draw from the biblical foundation that all individuals are equally valued in the eyes of God. They point to passages such as Galatians 3:28, which states, "There is neither Jew nor Gentile, neither slave nor free, nor is there male and female, for you are all one in Christ Jesus." This principle challenges societal hierarchies and distinctions.

2. **Imago Dei and Inherent Dignity:**
   - Christian anarchists emphasize the concept of Imago Dei, the belief that all humans are created in the image of God. This intrinsic worth and dignity, shared by every

individual, challenge hierarchical structures that diminish the value of certain groups. It forms the basis for an anarchist vision rooted in the recognition of the equal worth of every person.

3. **Jesus' Inclusive Ministry:**
   - The inclusive ministry of Jesus serves as a model for Christian anarchists. They argue that Jesus' interactions with people from all walks of life, including the marginalized and outcasts, underscore the radical equality inherent in the Christian message, challenging hierarchical societal norms.

4. **Rejecting Human-Created Hierarchies:**
   - Christian anarchists contend that human-created hierarchies, whether in government, social structures, or institutions, contradict the biblical principle of radical equality. They argue for a rejection of systems that perpetuate unequal power dynamics, favoring a society where authority is decentralized and based on mutual respect.

5. **Equality as a Kingdom Principle:**
   - Christian anarchists align the concept of radical equality with the principles of the Kingdom of God preached by Jesus. They argue that hierarchical structures go against the values of love, justice, and equality inherent in the Kingdom, advocating for societal models that reflect these divine principles.

6. **Challenge to Power Imbalances:**
   - Christian anarchists see the biblical call to radical equality as a challenge to power imbalances. They argue that hierarchical structures often concentrate power in the hands of a few, perpetuating injustice. An anarchist vision seeks to distribute power more equitably among all individuals.

7. **Biblical Narrative of Liberation:**
   - Christian anarchists point to the biblical narrative of liberation, from the Exodus story to Jesus' liberation ministry. They argue that these narratives emphasize the breaking of oppressive structures and the establishment of

societies that reflect the liberating principles of God.

8. **Participation in God's Kingdom of Equality:**
   - Christian anarchists see the pursuit of radical equality as a form of participating in God's Kingdom on Earth. They argue that dismantling hierarchical structures aligns with the biblical vision of a society where all individuals are valued, irrespective of their social status.

9. **Challenging Discrimination and Exclusion:**
   - The concept of radical equality challenges discrimination and exclusion based on race, gender, socio-economic status, and other factors. Christian anarchists advocate for dismantling structures that perpetuate such discrimination, fostering an inclusive society based on biblical principles.

10. **Anarchist Vision as a Response to Injustice:**

- Christian anarchists view the anarchist vision of a society without coercive authority as a response to societal injustices that arise from hierarchical structures. They argue that embracing radical equality aligns with biblical values and serves as a means to address systemic inequalities and promote a more just and equitable community.

30

Emphasizing Jesus' nonviolent resistance to oppressive systems, Christian anarchists contend that his example encourages believers to reject violent and coercive structures, advocating for alternative, non-hierarchical forms of community governance. Here's an exploration of this perspective:

1. **Jesus' Nonviolent Teachings:**
   - Christian anarchists highlight Jesus' explicit teachings on nonviolence, such as the Sermon on the Mount (Matthew 5-7), where he encourages turning the other cheek, loving enemies, and overcoming evil with good. They argue that these teachings provide a

foundation for rejecting violent means in addressing societal issues.

2. **Jesus' Actions as Nonviolent Resistance:**
   - Christian anarchists view Jesus' actions, including his refusal to respond violently to his own arrest and crucifixion, as a form of nonviolent resistance. They argue that Jesus' life serves as a powerful example of confronting oppressive systems without resorting to violence.

3. **Challenge to the Domination System:**
   - Jesus' nonviolent resistance is seen by Christian anarchists as a direct challenge to the domination system of his time. By refusing to engage in the cycle of violence, Jesus undermined the legitimacy of coercive structures and demonstrated an alternative way to address injustice.

4. **Rejecting the Sword:**
   - Christian anarchists draw attention to Jesus' statement, "Put your sword back into its place; for all who take the sword will

perish by the sword" (Matthew 26:52). They argue that this rebuke of violence reinforces the call to reject coercive structures, favoring nonviolent alternatives.

5. **Promoting a Culture of Peace:**
   - Christian anarchists advocate for the promotion of a culture of peace based on Jesus' example. They argue that his commitment to nonviolence encourages believers to actively work toward the establishment of communities and societies that prioritize peaceful resolutions to conflicts.

6. **Nonviolent Resistance to Systemic Injustices:**
   - Christian anarchists extend the concept of nonviolent resistance beyond personal interactions to systemic injustices. They contend that Jesus' confrontation with religious and political authorities without resorting to violence sets a precedent for addressing structural oppression through nonviolent means.

7. **Dismantling Power Hierarchies:**
   - Christian anarchists emphasize Jesus' nonviolent approach as a means of dismantling power hierarchies. They argue that coercive structures often rely on violence to maintain authority, and adopting a nonviolent stance challenges the foundations of hierarchical governance.

8. **Alternative Forms of Community Governance:**
   - Inspired by Jesus' nonviolent resistance, Christian anarchists advocate for alternative forms of community governance. They argue that hierarchical structures perpetuate violence and coercion, whereas non-hierarchical models encourage cooperative decision-making, consensus-building, and mutual respect.

9. **Solidarity with the Marginalized:**
   - Jesus' nonviolent resistance aligned with his solidarity with the marginalized. Christian anarchists argue that adopting nonviolent means allows believers to stand in solidarity with those oppressed by coercive structures,

promoting justice and equality without perpetuating harm.

10. **Active Peacemaking:**
   - Christian anarchists view Jesus' nonviolent resistance as a call to active peacemaking. They argue that believers are called to actively work toward the transformation of societies, dismantling coercive structures and fostering environments where peace, justice, and nonviolence prevail.

In summary, Christian anarchists emphasize Jesus' nonviolent resistance to oppressive systems as a guiding principle for believers. They contend that his example encourages the rejection of violent and coercive structures, fostering a commitment to alternative, non-hierarchical forms of community governance rooted in the principles of peace, justice, and love.

31

Building on the early Christian communal model, Christian anarchists advocate for a community-centered economy that emphasizes shared resources, mutual aid, and cooperative decision-making, aligning with biblical principles of communal well-being. Here's an exploration of this perspective:

1. **Early Christian Communal Model:**
   - Christian anarchists draw inspiration from the accounts in the book of Acts (Acts 2:44-47) that describe the early Christian community sharing resources, supporting one another, and living in harmony. They argue that this biblical model provides a blueprint for a community-centered economy.

2. **Emphasis on Shared Resources:**
   - Christian anarchists advocate for a departure from individualistic economic models, emphasizing the biblical principle of shared resources. They argue that a community-centered economy should prioritize collective ownership and distribution of resources to meet the needs of all community members.

3. **Mutual Aid as a Guiding Principle:**
   - Building on the biblical concept of mutual aid, Christian anarchists stress the importance of communities actively supporting each other. They contend that a community-centered economy should be characterized by a willingness to assist those in need, fostering a spirit of solidarity and care.

4. **Cooperative Decision-Making:**
   - Christian anarchists propose cooperative decision-making as an essential aspect of a community-centered economy. They argue that biblical principles encourage communities to engage in collective decision-making processes, ensuring that everyone has a voice in shaping the economic structure of the community.

5. **Rejecting Economic Exploitation:**
   - Christian anarchists see the early Christian communal model as a rejection of economic exploitation. They contend that a community-centered economy should actively work against systems that exploit individuals for

profit and instead prioritize equitable distribution of resources for the well-being of all.

6. **Biblical Principles of Communal Well-Being:**
   - Christian anarchists align their vision with biblical principles that emphasize communal well-being. They argue that a community-centered economy is rooted in the teachings of Jesus, where love, compassion, and care for one another are central to the community's economic practices.

7. **Resisting Greed and Accumulation:**
   - Drawing from biblical critiques of greed and accumulation, Christian anarchists advocate for an economic system that resists the excessive pursuit of wealth. They argue that a community-centered economy should prioritize the needs of the community over individual accumulation, aligning with biblical principles.

8. **Eradicating Poverty and Injustice:**

- Christian anarchists contend that a community-centered economy has the potential to eradicate poverty and social injustice. They argue that by actively sharing resources and practicing mutual aid, communities can address systemic inequalities and promote a more just and equitable society.

9. **Stewardship of God's Creation:**
   - Christian anarchists emphasize the biblical call to stewardship of God's creation. They argue that a community-centered economy should incorporate sustainable practices that prioritize environmental responsibility, reflecting the biblical mandate to care for the Earth.

10. **Encouraging Interdependence:**
   - Christian anarchists promote interdependence within communities as a key aspect of a community-centered economy. They argue that mutual support fosters stronger bonds among community members, creating a network of relationships that

prioritize the well-being of the entire community.

In summary, building on the early Christian communal model, Christian anarchists advocate for a community-centered economy that aligns with biblical principles of shared resources, mutual aid, and cooperative decision-making. They see this vision as a practical expression of communal well-being, rooted in the teachings of Jesus and the early Christian community described in the Bible.

32

Christian anarchists draw on biblical critiques of greed and the dangers of wealth accumulation, arguing that an anarchist approach, which prioritizes community over individual prosperity, reflects the biblical call to resist the pitfalls of excessive materialism. Here's an exploration of this perspective:

1. **Biblical Warnings Against Greed:**
   - Christian anarchists point to various biblical passages that explicitly warn against

the dangers of greed. Scriptures such as 1 Timothy 6:10, which states that the love of money is the root of all evil, serve as a foundation for their critique of wealth accumulation.

2. **Jesus' Teachings on Wealth:**
   - Christian anarchists emphasize Jesus' teachings on wealth, including his cautionary statements about the difficulty for the rich to enter the Kingdom of God (Matthew 19:23-24). They argue that these teachings underscore the biblical call to resist the allure of excessive materialism.

3. **Rejecting the Idolatry of Wealth:**
   - Drawing on the biblical theme of rejecting the idolatry of wealth, Christian anarchists argue that an anarchist approach prioritizes community well-being over individual prosperity. They contend that excessive materialism can become a substitute for a deeper spiritual connection and adherence to biblical principles.

4. **Economic Exploitation and Injustice:**

- Christian anarchists see the biblical critique of greed as intertwined with concerns about economic exploitation and injustice. They argue that an anarchist approach, by de-emphasizing individual prosperity and advocating for communal well-being, aligns with biblical principles of justice and fairness.

5. **Community-Centered Stewardship:**
   - Christian anarchists advocate for a community-centered approach to stewardship. They contend that biblical principles call for responsible and equitable use of resources within a community context, discouraging the accumulation of wealth that may lead to imbalances and inequalities.

6. **Prioritizing Love and Compassion:**
   - The biblical emphasis on love and compassion serves as a guiding principle for Christian anarchists. They argue that an anarchist approach, by prioritizing community needs over individual wealth, reflects the biblical call to love one's neighbor and actively care for those in need.

7. **Challenging Systems of Economic Injustice:**
   - Christian anarchists view the critique of greed as a call to challenge systems of economic injustice. They argue that an anarchist perspective, by resisting wealth accumulation and advocating for communal well-being, aligns with the biblical mandate to address systemic issues that perpetuate poverty and inequality.

8. **Biblical Examples of Generosity:**
   - Christian anarchists draw on biblical examples of generosity, such as the early Christian community in Acts 4:32-35, where believers shared their possessions. They argue that an anarchist approach encourages a culture of generosity and mutual support, reflecting the biblical ideal of communal sharing.

9. **Rejecting Mammon and Serving God:**
   - Christian anarchists reference Jesus' teaching that one cannot serve both God and Mammon (Matthew 6:24). They argue that an anarchist approach, by prioritizing

community over individual prosperity, aligns
with the biblical call to serve God rather than
the pursuit of wealth.

10. **Promoting a Culture of Contentment:**
   - Christian anarchists advocate for a culture
of contentment, drawing from biblical
teachings on finding satisfaction in God
rather than material possessions. They argue
that an anarchist approach fosters
contentment by shifting the focus from
individual accumulation to communal well-
being.

In summary, Christian anarchists draw on
biblical critiques of greed and the dangers of
wealth accumulation to argue for an anarchist
approach that prioritizes community over
individual prosperity. They see this
perspective as a reflection of the biblical call
to resist excessive materialism, promote
justice, and prioritize communal well-being.

33

Christian anarchists promote the concept of Sabbath economics, inspired by biblical principles of rest and renewal. They argue for economic systems that prioritize restorative justice, providing equitable opportunities, and addressing historical injustices. Here's an exploration of this perspective:

1. **Biblical Foundation of Sabbath Economics:**
   - Christian anarchists draw inspiration from the biblical concept of Sabbath, a day of rest and renewal, as outlined in the Ten Commandments (Exodus 20:8-11). They extend this principle to economics, proposing a system that incorporates cycles of rest, restoration, and justice.

2. **Sabbath as a Model for Economic Justice:**
   - Christian anarchists view the Sabbath as a model for economic justice, emphasizing the biblical call to provide rest not only for individuals but also for the entire community. They argue that Sabbath economics goes

beyond individual rest to address systemic inequalities and historical injustices.

3. **Equitable Distribution of Resources:**
   - Christian anarchists advocate for an equitable distribution of resources as a key component of Sabbath economics. They argue that economic systems should ensure that resources are shared fairly, promoting communal well-being and preventing the concentration of wealth in the hands of a few.

4. **Addressing Historical Injustices:**
   - Christian anarchists emphasize the need for Sabbath economics to address historical injustices. They argue that economic systems should actively work towards rectifying past wrongs, acknowledging disparities created by colonialism, slavery, and other forms of exploitation.

5. **Promoting Restorative Justice:**
   - Restorative justice is a central theme in Sabbath economics for Christian anarchists. They argue that economic systems should not only seek punishment for wrongdoing but

actively work towards restoring balance and healing the wounds caused by systemic injustices.

6. **Breaking Cycles of Exploitation:**
   - Christian anarchists see Sabbath economics as a way to break cycles of exploitation. They argue that by incorporating principles of rest and restoration, economic systems can disrupt patterns of oppression and create opportunities for marginalized communities to thrive.

7. **Reimagining Work and Productivity:**
   - Sabbath economics encourages a reimagining of work and productivity. Christian anarchists argue that economic systems should prioritize meaningful work, promote a healthy work-life balance, and avoid exploitative practices that lead to overwork and burnout.

8. **Community-Based Decision-Making:**
   - Christian anarchists propose community-based decision-making as an essential aspect of Sabbath economics. They argue that

communities should actively participate in shaping economic policies, ensuring that decisions align with principles of justice, equity, and communal well-being.

9. **Holistic Understanding of Sabbath:**
   - Sabbath economics for Christian anarchists involves a holistic understanding of Sabbath beyond a day of rest. They argue that it extends to economic structures that prioritize the holistic well-being of individuals, communities, and the environment.

10. **Environmental Stewardship:**
   - Christian anarchists link Sabbath economics with environmental stewardship. They argue that economic systems should prioritize sustainable practices, reflecting the biblical mandate to care for God's creation and ensuring that future generations inherit a healthy planet.

In summary, Christian anarchists promote Sabbath economics as a transformative approach inspired by biblical principles of rest and renewal. They argue for economic systems that prioritize restorative justice, address historical injustices, and create a framework for equitable opportunities and communal well-being.

34

Pointing to biblical covenants as models for community relationships, Christian anarchists argue for decentralized, voluntary associations based on mutual agreements and shared values, rejecting top-down authority structures in favor of consensual cooperation. Here's an exploration of this perspective:

1. **Biblical Foundation of Covenants:**
   - Christian anarchists draw inspiration from biblical covenants, such as the covenant with Noah, Abraham, and the covenant at Sinai. They view these agreements as models for how communities can be organized based on mutual consent and shared values.

2. **Voluntary Nature of Biblical Covenants:**

- Christian anarchists highlight the voluntary nature of biblical covenants, emphasizing that individuals and communities entered into these agreements willingly. They argue that this voluntary aspect serves as a foundation for rejecting coercive authority structures in favor of consensual cooperation.

3. **Decentralization in Biblical Covenants:**
   - The decentralized nature of biblical covenants is a key theme for Christian anarchists. They point to instances where God establishes direct relationships with individuals or smaller groups, avoiding centralized authority. This decentralized model aligns with their vision of community organization.

4. **Mutual Agreements and Shared Values:**
   - Christian anarchists argue for decentralized, voluntary associations formed through mutual agreements and shared values. They believe that communities should

be based on consensual cooperation, where individuals come together willingly, sharing common principles and goals.

5. **Rejecting Top-Down Authority:**
   - Christian anarchists explicitly reject top-down authority structures, drawing from the biblical model of covenants. They argue that top-down authority contradicts the voluntary and consensual nature of biblical covenants, and communities should instead be organized through participatory decision-making.

6. **Consensual Cooperation in Community Governance:**
   - Christian anarchists advocate for consensual cooperation in community governance, where decisions are made collectively and everyone has a voice. They argue that this approach reflects the biblical principles of mutual respect and shared responsibility found in covenantal relationships.

7. **Equality and Shared Responsibility:**

- Christian anarchists emphasize the equality and shared responsibility inherent in biblical covenants. They argue that communities based on consensual cooperation should prioritize these principles, ensuring that no individual or group exerts disproportionate influence over others.

8. **Dynamic and Adaptable Communities:**
   - Drawing inspiration from biblical covenants that adapted to changing circumstances, Christian anarchists envision dynamic and adaptable communities. They argue that consensual cooperation allows for flexibility and responsiveness to the evolving needs and challenges faced by the community.

9. **Emphasis on Personal Responsibility:**
   - Christian anarchists stress the importance of personal responsibility within consensually organized communities. They argue that individuals voluntarily commit to shared values and responsibilities, fostering a sense

of accountability without the need for external authority.

10. **Biblical Examples of Covenantal Communities:**
   - Christian anarchists point to biblical examples of covenantal communities, such as the early Christian community described in Acts 2:44-47. They argue that these communities exemplified consensual cooperation, voluntary sharing, and decentralized decision-making.

In summary, Christian anarchists look to biblical covenants as models for community relationships, advocating for decentralized, voluntary associations based on mutual agreements and shared values. They reject top-down authority structures in favor of consensual cooperation, aligning their vision with biblical principles of voluntary commitment, equality, and shared responsibility.

35

Christian anarchists draw inspiration from biblical calls to resist conforming to worldly patterns. They argue that embracing an anarchist perspective allows believers to resist cultural conformity and prioritize adherence to the ethical teachings of Jesus. Here's an exploration of this perspective:

1. **Biblical Exhortations Against Conformity:**
   - Christian anarchists point to biblical passages such as Romans 12:2, which urges believers not to conform to the patterns of this world but to be transformed by the renewing of their minds. They interpret this as a call to resist societal norms that contradict the teachings of Jesus.

2. **Challenge to Status Quo:**
   - Embracing an anarchist perspective represents a challenge to the status quo for Christian anarchists. They argue that conformity to worldly systems often perpetuates injustice, inequality, and oppression, whereas embracing alternative

perspectives allows for transformative change.

3. **Alignment with Counter-Cultural Values:**
   - Christian anarchists see their rejection of cultural conformity as aligning with the counter-cultural values espoused by Jesus. They argue that Jesus' teachings challenged the prevailing norms of his time and called for a radical transformation of society based on love, justice, and compassion.

4. **Prioritizing Kingdom Values:**
   - By resisting conformity to worldly patterns, Christian anarchists prioritize adherence to the values of the Kingdom of God. They argue that embracing an anarchist perspective allows believers to align their actions with the ethical teachings of Jesus, promoting love, peace, and equality.

5. **Freedom from Cultural Influences:**
   - Christian anarchists advocate for freedom from cultural influences that may lead believers away from their faith or

compromise their commitment to following Jesus. They argue that embracing an anarchist perspective allows individuals to critically examine societal norms and choose paths that reflect their faith convictions.

6. **Rejecting Consumerism and Materialism:**
   - An anarchist perspective encourages believers to reject the consumerist and materialistic values often promoted by worldly systems. Christian anarchists argue that prioritizing simplicity, community, and service over material possessions reflects the teachings of Jesus and resists the cultural obsession with wealth and consumption.

7. **Championing Nonviolent Resistance:**
   - Christian anarchists champion nonviolent resistance to oppressive systems as a way to resist conformity to worldly patterns of violence and coercion. They argue that Jesus' example of nonviolent resistance offers a powerful alternative to the dominant culture's reliance on force and domination.

8. **Fostering Authentic Christian Witness:**
   - By resisting cultural conformity, Christian anarchists aim to foster an authentic Christian witness in the world. They argue that embracing anarchist principles allows believers to embody the radical love, compassion, and justice exemplified by Jesus, thereby bearing witness to the transformative power of the Gospel.

9. **Promoting Alternative Communities:**
   - Christian anarchists promote the creation of alternative communities that challenge cultural norms and embody Kingdom values. They argue that these communities serve as beacons of light in a world darkened by conformity, offering hope and inspiration to those seeking an alternative way of life.

10. **Empowering Individual and Collective Action:**
   - Embracing an anarchist perspective empowers individuals and communities to take meaningful action against injustice and oppression. Christian anarchists argue that by

resisting cultural conformity and embracing alternative perspectives, believers can work towards building a more just, equitable, and compassionate world in alignment with the teachings of Jesus.

In summary, Christian anarchists draw inspiration from biblical calls to resist conforming to worldly patterns, advocating for an alternative perspective that prioritizes adherence to the ethical teachings of Jesus. They see embracing an anarchist perspective as a means of challenging cultural norms, promoting Kingdom values, and fostering authentic Christian witness in the world.

36

Christian anarchists see the call to subvert empire-like structures with servant leadership as a biblical mandate. They argue that leaders should be chosen based on their willingness to serve rather than through hierarchical positions imposed by authority. Here's an exploration of this perspective:

1. **Biblical Foundation of Servant Leadership:**
   - Christian anarchists point to Jesus' teachings on servant leadership as a foundational aspect of their perspective. They highlight passages such as Matthew 20:25-28, where Jesus explicitly contrasts the leadership style of the world with that of his followers, emphasizing service and humility.

2. **Rejecting Hierarchical Positions:**
   - Christian anarchists reject the idea of leaders being chosen based on hierarchical positions imposed by authority. They argue that hierarchical structures often perpetuate power imbalances and can lead to exploitation, and instead, advocate for leaders who emerge through a commitment to serving others.

3. **Imitating Jesus' Example:**
   - Christian anarchists see Jesus' own life as the embodiment of servant leadership. They argue that by imitating Jesus' example of washing the disciples' feet and prioritizing the needs of others, leaders can subvert

traditional, empire-like structures that rely on domination and control.

4. **Equating Leadership with Service:**
   - Christian anarchists equate true leadership with service. They argue that leaders, in the spirit of servant leadership, should prioritize the well-being of those they lead, fostering an environment of mutual care and support rather than one driven by authority and control.

5. **Resisting the Temptation of Power:**
   - Servant leadership, according to Christian anarchists, involves resisting the temptation of power. They argue that leaders should actively reject the allure of hierarchical authority and focus on serving others selflessly, mirroring the humility exemplified by Jesus.

6. **Egalitarian Community Structure:**
   - Christian anarchists advocate for an egalitarian community structure where leadership emerges organically from a commitment to service. They argue that this

approach challenges the authoritarian tendencies of traditional leadership models and fosters a sense of shared responsibility within the community.

7. **Leadership by Example:**
   - Servant leadership, for Christian anarchists, involves leading by example. They argue that leaders should embody the values they espouse, actively engaging in acts of service and humility to inspire others within the community to follow a similar path.

8. **Promoting Collective Decision-Making:**
   - Christian anarchists argue for collective decision-making processes rather than decisions imposed by a hierarchical authority. They believe that a servant leadership model encourages collaborative efforts and values the input of all community members in decision-making processes.

9. **Caring for the Marginalized:**

- Servant leadership, as advocated by Christian anarchists, involves a special focus on caring for the marginalized and vulnerable. They argue that leaders should prioritize the needs of those on the margins of society, reflecting Jesus' concern for the oppressed.

10. **Creating Empowering Environments:**
   - Christian anarchists envision servant leaders creating empowering environments. They argue that leaders should work towards fostering a sense of agency and empowerment among community members, allowing individuals to contribute their unique gifts and talents for the collective good.

In summary, Christian anarchists see the call to subvert empire-like structures with servant leadership as a biblical mandate. They argue for leaders chosen based on their willingness to serve, rejecting hierarchical positions imposed by authority in favor of a leadership style that prioritizes humility, mutual care, and collective well-being.

37

Building on the biblical principles of peace and nonviolence, Christian anarchists advocate for pacifism and the rejection of state violence. They argue that an anarchist society aligns with Jesus' teachings of turning the other cheek and loving enemies. Here's an exploration of this perspective:

1. **Biblical Foundations of Peace and Nonviolence:**
   - Christian anarchists draw inspiration from biblical principles that promote peace and nonviolence. They point to passages such as Matthew 5:9, where Jesus pronounces blessings on peacemakers, and Matthew 5:38-48, which includes the teachings of turning the other cheek and loving enemies.

2. **Rejecting State Violence:**
   - Christian anarchists argue for the rejection of state violence, emphasizing that the use of

force by governing authorities contradicts the teachings of Jesus. They contend that an anarchist society, built on voluntary cooperation and mutual aid, stands in contrast to the coercive nature of state power.

3. **Pacifism as a Christian Ethic:**
   - Christian anarchists advocate for pacifism as a central Christian ethic. They argue that Jesus' example and teachings, along with the broader biblical narrative, promote the resolution of conflicts through nonviolent means, and followers of Christ should embody this ethic in all aspects of life.

4. **Nonviolent Resistance to Injustice:**
   - Christian anarchists promote nonviolent resistance to injustice as a practical application of Jesus' teachings. They argue that an anarchist society, rooted in the principles of peace and nonviolence, provides a framework for addressing societal issues without resorting to state-sponsored violence.

5. **Turning the Other Cheek:**

- The concept of turning the other cheek, as taught by Jesus in Matthew 5:39, is central to the pacifist stance of Christian anarchists. They argue that an anarchist society encourages individuals to respond to aggression with nonviolent resistance, seeking reconciliation rather than retaliation.

6. **Loving Enemies:**
   - Christian anarchists emphasize the radical call to love enemies, a teaching found in Matthew 5:44. They argue that this principle challenges the notion of justifying violence against perceived adversaries and instead promotes a commitment to reconciliation, forgiveness, and transformative love.

7. **Preventing the Cycle of Violence:**
   - Christian anarchists assert that rejecting state violence and embracing pacifism helps prevent the perpetuation of a cycle of violence. They argue that an anarchist society, by refusing to employ coercive force, creates an environment where conflicts can be resolved through dialogue and understanding rather than through aggression.

8. **Promoting a Culture of Peace:**
   - An anarchist society, according to Christian anarchists, promotes a culture of peace. They argue that when individuals and communities prioritize nonviolence, mutual aid, and cooperation, they contribute to the creation of environments that nurture harmony and understanding.

9. **Advocating Disarmament:**
   - Christian anarchists advocate for disarmament as part of their commitment to pacifism. They argue that the dismantling of military structures aligns with the biblical call to beat swords into plowshares (Isaiah 2:4) and redirects resources towards the well-being of communities rather than perpetuating violence.

10. **Seeking Restorative Justice:**
   - Christian anarchists emphasize the pursuit of restorative justice over punitive measures. They argue that an anarchist society, grounded in the principles of peace and nonviolence, seeks to address harm through

reconciliation, healing, and rebuilding relationships rather than through punitive actions.

In summary, building on the biblical principles of peace and nonviolence, Christian anarchists advocate for pacifism and the rejection of state violence. They contend that an anarchist society aligns with Jesus' teachings, promoting a culture of peace, nonviolent resistance, and the transformative love that seeks reconciliation even with enemies.

38

Christian anarchists highlight the biblical emphasis on voluntary cooperation, drawing from passages that encourage believers to freely contribute and cooperate for the common good. They argue that an anarchist framework allows for the organic development of cooperative, voluntary communities. Here's an exploration of this perspective:

1. **Biblical Foundations of Voluntary Cooperation:**
   - Christian anarchists point to biblical passages that emphasize voluntary cooperation, such as 2 Corinthians 9:7, where believers are encouraged to give willingly and cheerfully. They argue that these principles lay the foundation for a community based on voluntary collaboration.

2. **Freedom in Giving and Sharing:**
   - Christian anarchists see the biblical emphasis on voluntary cooperation as reflective of the freedom found in giving and sharing. They argue that individuals should be free to contribute their resources, talents, and efforts willingly, fostering a spirit of generosity and mutual aid.

3. **Acts of Voluntary Community Support:**
   - The book of Acts serves as a key reference for Christian anarchists, particularly Acts 2:44-45, where early believers voluntarily shared their possessions and resources. They argue that this example

showcases the organic development of a cooperative community based on voluntary contributions.

4. **Rejecting Coercive Structures:**
   - Christian anarchists reject coercive structures in favor of voluntary cooperation. They argue that attempts to enforce cooperation through authority or hierarchy go against the biblical principles of generosity and voluntary giving, which are central to the formation of genuine community bonds.

5. **Communal Living in Acts:**
   - Christian anarchists draw inspiration from the communal living described in Acts 4:32-37, where believers voluntarily shared their resources for the well-being of the community. They argue that this cooperative model is consistent with the principles of anarchism, emphasizing voluntary collaboration over imposed authority.

6. **Creating Spaces for Voluntary Contributions:**

- An anarchist framework, according to Christian anarchists, creates spaces where individuals can voluntarily contribute to the community based on their abilities and resources. They argue that this approach encourages a sense of ownership and responsibility within the community.

7. **Non-Coercive Decision-Making:**
   - Christian anarchists advocate for non-coercive decision-making processes within communities. They argue that decisions should be made collectively, with individuals freely participating based on their convictions, rather than being coerced into compliance with authoritative structures.

8. **Mutual Aid as a Core Principle:**
   - Christian anarchists see mutual aid as a core principle derived from biblical teachings. They argue that voluntary cooperation for the common good is exemplified in acts of mutual aid, where individuals willingly support and assist one another without external coercion.

9. **Celebrating Diverse Contributions:**
   - In an anarchist framework, Christian anarchists celebrate the diverse contributions individuals can make voluntarily. They argue that the Bible's emphasis on the unique gifts and talents of believers encourages a community where diverse skills and resources are freely offered for the benefit of all.

10. **Encouraging Participatory Community Building:**
   - Christian anarchists encourage participatory community building, where individuals actively engage in shaping the community's direction. They argue that this approach allows for the organic growth of a community based on shared values and the voluntary cooperation of its members.

In summary, Christian anarchists highlight the biblical emphasis on voluntary cooperation, drawing from passages that encourage believers to freely contribute and cooperate for the common good. They argue that an anarchist framework provides the foundation for the organic development of cooperative, voluntary communities, aligning with the principles of generosity, mutual aid, and shared responsibility found in the Bible.

39

Christian anarchists argue that the biblical emphasis on humility, exemplified by Jesus washing the disciples' feet, supports an anarchist perspective that rejects hierarchical power structures in favor of servant leadership. Here's an exploration of this perspective:

1. **Jesus' Act of Foot Washing as a Symbol of Humility:**
   - Christian anarchists highlight the significant event in the New Testament where Jesus, despite being a revered teacher and leader, humbly washes the feet of his disciples (John 13:1-17). This act is seen as a powerful symbol of humility, challenging traditional notions of authority and hierarchy.

2. **Rejecting Worldly Notions of Leadership:**

- Christian anarchists draw from Jesus' teachings that contrast the leadership style of the world with that of his followers (Matthew 20:25-28). They argue that this rejection of worldly notions of leadership aligns with anarchist ideals, emphasizing a servant-hearted approach over authoritarian control.

3. **Servant Leadership as a Biblical Mandate:**
   - Christian anarchists contend that the call to servant leadership is a biblical mandate derived from Jesus' example. They argue that leaders should follow Jesus' footsteps in serving others, fostering a community based on mutual care, cooperation, and a rejection of top-down authority.

4. **Challenging Hierarchical Structures:**
   - The act of foot washing challenges hierarchical structures, according to Christian anarchists. They argue that Jesus intentionally chose a menial task to emphasize that leadership is about service and not about holding positions of power over others.

5. **Empowering Through Humility:**
   - Christian anarchists assert that humility is empowering. By rejecting hierarchical power structures, leaders can empower others to contribute freely and participate in decision-making processes, fostering a sense of shared responsibility within the community.

6. **Community-Based Decision-Making:**
   - Anarchist principles of decentralized decision-making resonate with the biblical emphasis on humility. Christian anarchists argue for community-based decision-making processes where individuals collectively discern and contribute to the well-being of the community, promoting equality and humility.

7. **Imitating Jesus' Radical Example:**
   - Christian anarchists see imitating Jesus' radical example of humility as a central tenet of their faith. They argue that this imitation extends to rejecting hierarchical structures and promoting a leadership style rooted in service and love.

8. **Embracing Voluntary Cooperation:**

- Anarchist principles of voluntary cooperation find support in Jesus' humble actions. Christian anarchists argue that individuals should voluntarily collaborate for the common good, emphasizing the importance of mutual aid and cooperation over imposed authority.

9. **Fostering Inclusivity:**
   - Christian anarchists emphasize the inclusivity embedded in servant leadership. They argue that by rejecting hierarchical power dynamics, leaders create an environment where everyone feels valued and included, fostering a sense of community and belonging.

10. **Building a Culture of Mutual Respect:**
   - Servant leadership, according to Christian anarchists, builds a culture of mutual respect within communities. They argue that leaders, by embracing humility, model a respect for the dignity of every individual, cultivating an atmosphere of trust and cooperation.

11. **Promoting Non-Coercive Leadership:**
   - Christian anarchists advocate for non-coercive leadership. They argue that servant leadership, rooted in humility, rejects the use of force or authority to control others, creating space for individuals to contribute willingly and participate in decision-making without external coercion.

12. **Aligning Leadership with Jesus' Teachings:**
- Ultimately, Christian anarchists contend that the rejection of hierarchical power structures and the embrace of servant leadership align with the core teachings of Jesus. They argue that this perspective fosters communities based on love, humility, and a commitment to serving one another, mirroring the example set by Christ.

40

Christian anarchists advocate for community-based decision-making processes, drawing inspiration from the early Christian communities described in Acts. They argue that this model reflects an anarchist approach where decisions are made collectively, fostering a sense of equality and shared responsibility. Here's an exploration of this perspective:

1. **Biblical Basis in Acts 2:44-45:**
   - Christian anarchists point to the early Christian communities described in Acts 2:44-45, where believers shared everything in common and distributed resources based on need. They argue that this biblical example serves as a foundation for community-based decision-making.

2. **Rejecting Authoritarian Structures:**
   - Christian anarchists reject authoritarian decision-making structures, drawing from Jesus' teachings on servant leadership. They argue that hierarchical models of decision-making contradict the principles of equality and shared responsibility found in the Bible.

3. **Collective Wisdom and Discernment:**

- Advocates of community-based decision-making emphasize the importance of collective wisdom and discernment. They argue that decisions made in community reflect a diversity of perspectives, enhancing the quality of choices and ensuring that the entire community's needs are considered.

4. **Fostering a Spirit of Inclusivity:**
   - Christian anarchists stress the inclusivity inherent in community-based decision-making. They argue that this approach allows for the participation of all community members, irrespective of social status or position, fostering a sense of inclusivity and egalitarianism.

5. **Decentralization of Power:**
   - Anarchist principles advocate for the decentralization of power, and Christian anarchists apply this concept to decision-making. They argue that distributing decision-making authority among community members prevents the concentration of power in the hands of a few, promoting a more equitable distribution of influence.

6. **Reflecting the Kingdom of God:**
   - Christian anarchists contend that community-based decision-making reflects the values of the Kingdom of God. They argue that such a model aligns with Jesus' teachings on humility, servanthood, and the importance of considering the needs of others.

7. **Consensus-Building and Cooperation:**
   - Anarchist principles emphasize consensus-building and cooperation as essential elements of decision-making. Christian anarchists argue that these principles are reflected in the communal decision-making processes described in Acts, where believers worked together for the common good.

8. **Accountability and Shared Responsibility:**
   - Community-based decision-making promotes accountability and shared responsibility. Christian anarchists argue that when decisions are made collectively, each

member of the community is accountable to the others, fostering a sense of shared responsibility for the outcomes.

9. **Participatory Democracy in Action:**
   - Christian anarchists see community-based decision-making as a form of participatory democracy in action. They argue that this approach allows all members to have a voice and a vote, fostering a sense of ownership and engagement in the community's affairs.

10. **Resolving Conflicts Through Dialogue:**
   - Anarchist principles advocate for resolving conflicts through dialogue and consensus rather than coercion. Christian anarchists argue that community-based decision-making provides a framework for addressing disagreements peacefully, promoting reconciliation and understanding.

11. **Adaptability to Local Contexts:**
   - Community-based decision-making, according to Christian anarchists, allows for adaptability to local contexts. They argue that

decisions made within the community take into account the unique needs and circumstances of its members, promoting a more flexible and responsive governance model.

12. **Reflecting Mutual Aid and Interconnectedness:**
   - Christian anarchists connect community-based decision-making to the biblical principle of mutual aid and interconnectedness. They argue that this approach reflects the idea that individuals within a community are interconnected and mutually responsible for each other's well-being.

In summary, Christian anarchists advocate for community-based decision-making processes, drawing inspiration from the early Christian communities described in Acts. They argue that this model reflects an anarchist approach that values collective wisdom, rejects authoritarian structures, and fosters a sense of equality and shared responsibility within the community.

41

Christian anarchists align with the biblical call for social justice, emphasizing passages like Micah 6:8. They argue that an anarchist society, rooted in principles of justice and equity, is consistent with the biblical mandate to act justly, love mercy, and walk humbly with God. Here's an exploration of this perspective:

1. **Micah 6:8 as a Guiding Principle:**
   - Christian anarchists point to Micah 6:8, which states, "He has shown you, O mortal, what is good. And what does the Lord require of you? To act justly and to love mercy and to walk humbly with your God." This verse is seen as a foundational principle guiding believers toward a just and compassionate way of life.

2. **Acting Justly in an Anarchist Society:**
   - Advocates of Christian anarchism argue that an anarchist society allows individuals to actively pursue justice. They contend that by

rejecting hierarchical power structures, communities can establish more equitable systems that address social injustices and ensure fairness for all.

3. **Love and Mercy as Core Values:**
   - Christian anarchists emphasize the core values of love and mercy inherent in Micah 6:8. They argue that these values are foundational to an anarchist society, where mutual aid, compassion, and a commitment to the well-being of others are central to community life.

4. **Rejecting Coercive Measures:**
   - An anarchist perspective, according to Christian anarchists, aligns with the rejection of coercive measures. They argue that a society rooted in justice and mercy should avoid the imposition of authority through force, opting instead for voluntary cooperation and collective decision-making.

5. **Promoting Inclusivity and Equality:**
   - Christian anarchists assert that an anarchist society promotes inclusivity and

equality, key components of acting justly. They argue that by dismantling hierarchical structures, individuals can work toward a more just and inclusive community that values the dignity and worth of every person.

6. **Addressing Systemic Injustices:**
   - Anarchist principles, Christian anarchists argue, provide a framework for addressing systemic injustices. They contend that by challenging oppressive structures and advocating for decentralized, community-based solutions, individuals can work toward creating a more just and equitable society.

7. **Walking Humbly by Rejecting Arrogance:**
   - Walking humbly, as emphasized in Micah 6:8, is seen as a rejection of arrogance and oppressive authority. Christian anarchists argue that an anarchist society encourages humility by fostering a culture of shared responsibility, mutual respect, and the acknowledgment that no one person or group should hold undue power over others.

8. **Advocating for Economic Justice:**
   - Christian anarchists connect the call for social justice to economic justice. They argue that an anarchist approach, which prioritizes community well-being over individual prosperity, aligns with the biblical mandate to address economic disparities and ensure the fair distribution of resources.

9. **Rejecting Exploitative Practices:**
   - Anarchist principles, according to Christian anarchists, reject exploitative practices that lead to social inequalities. They argue that by dismantling hierarchical economic structures, individuals can create a society that values fairness, mutual support, and the well-being of all community members.

10. **Championing Nonviolent Resistance:**
   - Christian anarchists advocate for nonviolent resistance as a means to address social injustices. They argue that an anarchist society, rooted in principles of justice and equity, aligns with the biblical call to resist

oppression peacefully and work toward transformative change.

11. **Living Out Kingdom Values:**
   - Christian anarchists see an anarchist society as a way of living out the values of God's Kingdom on Earth. They argue that by embracing justice, mercy, and humility in community life, individuals can actively participate in building a society that reflects the principles outlined in Micah 6:8.

12. **Creating Spaces for Collective Empowerment:**
   - Anarchist principles, as advocated by Christian anarchists, create spaces for collective empowerment. They argue that by rejecting oppressive structures, individuals can work together to build communities where everyone has the opportunity to flourish, fostering a society rooted in justice and equity.

In summary, Christian anarchists align with the biblical call for social justice, emphasizing passages like Micah 6:8. They argue that an anarchist society, rooted in principles of justice and equity, is consistent with the biblical mandate to act justly, love mercy, and walk humbly with God.

42

Drawing from biblical warnings against idolatry, Christian anarchists argue against the deification of state authority. They contend that placing ultimate trust in the state contradicts the biblical call to worship God alone and can lead to the abuse of power. Here's an exploration of this perspective:

1. **Biblical Warnings Against Idolatry:**
   - Christian anarchists draw on numerous biblical passages warning against idolatry, emphasizing commandments such as "You shall have no other gods before me" (Exodus 20:3). They argue that idolizing the state can lead to a misplaced allegiance that conflicts with the central tenets of monotheism.

2. **State as a Potential Idol:**

- Christian anarchists view the deification of state authority as a potential idol that competes with the worship of God. They argue that when the state is elevated to a position of ultimate authority, it can lead to the prioritization of human-made institutions over divine principles.

3. **Contradiction to the First Commandment:**
   - Advocates of Christian anarchism assert that deifying state authority contradicts the first commandment, which emphasizes exclusive devotion to God. Placing ultimate trust in the state, they argue, undermines the foundational principle of monotheism and can lead to moral compromises.

4. **State as a Competing Allegiance:**
   - Christian anarchists argue that elevating the state to a position of deification creates a competing allegiance that diverts attention and devotion away from God. They contend that unwavering loyalty to the state may compromise the ethical standards and values upheld by biblical teachings.

5. **Abuse of Power and Authority:**
   - By warning against the deification of the state, Christian anarchists highlight the potential for the abuse of power and authority. They argue that when the state is treated as a quasi-divine entity, it becomes susceptible to corruption, authoritarianism, and actions that go against the principles of justice and compassion.

6. **State Worship as a Distraction:**
   - Christian anarchists contend that idolizing state authority can become a distraction from spiritual priorities. They argue that excessive focus on the state may lead individuals away from the core teachings of faith, as their allegiance becomes divided between God and the state.

7. **Perversion of Divine Principles:**
   - Christian anarchists express concern that the deification of the state can lead to the perversion of divine principles. They argue that when the state is granted ultimate authority, it may enact policies and practices

that contradict the moral imperatives outlined in the Bible.

8. **Rejection of Caesar as God:**
   - Christian anarchists reference biblical narratives, such as the account of Daniel refusing to worship King Darius, to emphasize the rejection of state leaders as objects of worship (Daniel 6:16-23). They argue that the same principle applies to modern states, cautioning against the elevation of political figures or institutions to divine status.

9. **Guarding Against Totalitarianism:**
   - Advocates of Christian anarchism see the rejection of state deification as a safeguard against totalitarianism. They argue that maintaining a clear distinction between the authority of the state and the ultimate authority of God helps prevent the concentration of power and the erosion of individual liberties.

10. **Promoting God-Centered Societal Values:**

- Christian anarchists advocate for a society centered around God's principles rather than the deification of state authority. They argue that aligning societal values with divine guidance fosters a more just, compassionate, and morally grounded community.

11. **Resisting Statolatry:**
    - The term "statolatry" is used by Christian anarchists to describe the worship of the state. They argue that resisting statolatry is essential for maintaining a faithful and morally upright society, in line with the biblical call to worship God alone.

12. **Cultivating Spiritual Discernment:**
    - Christian anarchists encourage individuals to cultivate spiritual discernment to distinguish between allegiance to the state and devotion to God. They argue that a clear understanding of the dangers of idolizing the state allows for a more faithful and God-centered approach to societal participation.

In summary, drawing from biblical warnings against idolatry, Christian anarchists argue against the deification of state authority. They contend that placing ultimate trust in the state contradicts the biblical call to worship God alone and can lead to the abuse of power, emphasizing the importance of maintaining a God-centered perspective in societal governance.

43

Christian anarchists extend the concept of Sabbath economics to include an economic Sabbath. They argue that economic systems should allow for periods of rest and renewal, aligning with biblical principles of Sabbath rest and economic justice. Here's an exploration of this perspective:

1. **Biblical Basis in the Sabbath Commandment:**
   - Christian anarchists draw from the biblical commandment to observe the Sabbath day as a day of rest, found in Exodus 20:8-11. They argue that this principle extends beyond

personal rest to encompass economic practices, emphasizing the need for periodic pauses in economic activity.

2. **Sabbath Economics as a Holistic Concept:**
   - Advocates of Christian anarchism view Sabbath economics as a holistic concept that encompasses not only personal rest but also systemic economic practices. They argue that economic Sabbath reflects the biblical idea that rest is not only an individual necessity but also a societal requirement.

3. **Restoring Balance to Economic Systems:**
   - Christian anarchists contend that an economic Sabbath is essential for restoring balance to economic systems. They argue that continuous economic activity without periods of rest can lead to exploitation, inequality, and environmental degradation, undermining the biblical call for stewardship and justice.

4. **Cycles of Rest and Renewal:**

- Drawing from the cyclical nature of the Sabbath, Christian anarchists advocate for cycles of rest and renewal within economic systems. They argue that these cycles allow for the rejuvenation of individuals, communities, and the environment, aligning with biblical principles of sustainability and responsible stewardship.

5. **Avoiding Exploitative Practices:**
   - Christian anarchists express concern that a lack of economic Sabbath may contribute to exploitative practices. They argue that unrelenting economic activity can lead to overwork, poverty, and the disregard for the well-being of workers, contradicting biblical principles of justice and compassion.

6. **Sabbatical Years and Jubilee:**
   - Referencing the biblical concepts of Sabbatical years and Jubilee found in Leviticus 25, Christian anarchists argue for economic Sabbath in the form of periodic rest for the land and the forgiveness of debts. They contend that these practices promote

economic justice, equality, and the redistribution of resources.

7. **Humanizing Economic Systems:**
   - Christian anarchists argue that incorporating economic Sabbath humanizes economic systems. They contend that by prioritizing rest, businesses, and institutions can create environments that value the holistic well-being of individuals, fostering healthier, more compassionate societies.

8. **Promoting Well-Being over Endless Growth:**
   - Advocates of economic Sabbath emphasize the prioritization of well-being over endless economic growth. They argue that an economic system driven solely by constant expansion can lead to environmental degradation, income inequality, and societal unrest, undermining the principles of economic justice found in the Bible.

9. **Sustainable Resource Management:**
   - Christian anarchists highlight the importance of sustainable resource

management within the concept of economic Sabbath. They argue that allowing the land and resources to rest periodically prevents depletion and environmental degradation, reflecting the biblical mandate to steward God's creation responsibly.

10. **Community-Building Through Shared Rest:**
   - Christian anarchists argue that economic Sabbath contributes to community-building. They contend that synchronized periods of rest allow communities to come together, share resources, and support one another, fostering a sense of solidarity and mutual aid in accordance with biblical teachings.

11. **Resisting Consumerism and Materialism:**
   - By promoting economic Sabbath, Christian anarchists argue for resistance against rampant consumerism and materialism. They contend that a cyclical approach to economic activity encourages individuals to focus on values beyond mere

consumption, aligning with biblical teachings on contentment and simplicity.

12. **Advocacy for Sabbatarian Economics:**
   - Christian anarchists advocate for a Sabbatarian approach to economics, where periodic rest and renewal are integrated into the fabric of economic systems. They argue that such an approach aligns with the biblical vision of a society that values justice, compassion, and the well-being of both individuals and the wider community.

In summary, Christian anarchists extend the concept of Sabbath economics to include an economic Sabbath, emphasizing the need for rest and renewal within economic systems. They argue that aligning economic practices with biblical principles of Sabbath rest and economic justice promotes a more humane, sustainable, and just society.

44

Christian anarchists draw from biblical critiques of injustice and oppression, such as Isaiah 58. They argue that anarchism provides a framework for actively resisting systemic injustice and working towards a more compassionate and equitable society. Here's an exploration of this perspective:

1. **Isaiah 58 as a Call to Action:**
   - Christian anarchists point to Isaiah 58 as a powerful biblical passage that addresses the relationship between religious rituals and social justice. The chapter challenges superficial acts of worship while calling for genuine compassion, justice, and the liberation of the oppressed.

2. **Anarchism as a Tool for Resistance:**
   - Advocates of Christian anarchism see anarchism as a framework that empowers individuals to actively resist systemic injustice. They argue that by rejecting hierarchical structures, individuals can challenge oppressive systems and work towards creating a society that aligns with the principles outlined in Isaiah 58.

3. **Critique of Empty Rituals:**
   - Christian anarchists draw parallels between Isaiah's critique of empty rituals and their critique of institutionalized structures that perpetuate injustice. They argue that both the biblical passage and anarchism call for a deeper, transformative engagement with the world, moving beyond mere symbolic gestures.

4. **Active Opposition to Exploitation:**
   - Drawing from Isaiah's call to "loose the chains of injustice" (Isaiah 58:6), Christian anarchists advocate for active opposition to systems that perpetuate exploitation. They argue that anarchism provides a means to dismantle oppressive structures and create alternative, just ways of organizing society.

5. **Empowering the Marginalized:**
   - Christian anarchists align with Isaiah's emphasis on caring for the marginalized and oppressed. They argue that anarchism, by rejecting authoritarian structures, empowers individuals and communities to address the

needs of the vulnerable, creating spaces for shared responsibility and mutual aid.

6. **Rejecting Systems of Oppression:**
   - Advocates of Christian anarchism contend that anarchism aligns with the biblical call to "break every yoke" (Isaiah 58:6), urging believers to reject systems of oppression. They argue that dismantling hierarchical structures allows for the elimination of unjust yokes that burden individuals and communities.

7. **Advocacy for Economic Justice:**
   - Christian anarchists connect Isaiah's call to share bread with the hungry and provide shelter to the homeless (Isaiah 58:7) with their advocacy for economic justice. They argue that anarchism provides a framework for challenging economic systems that perpetuate inequality and promoting equitable distribution of resources.

8. **Promotion of Mutual Aid:**
   - Anarchist principles, according to Christian anarchists, resonate with Isaiah's

call to "not turn away from your own flesh and blood" (Isaiah 58:7). They argue that anarchism promotes mutual aid and cooperation, fostering a community-centered approach to addressing the needs of individuals and ensuring that no one is turned away.

9. **Creating Just Communities:**
   - Christian anarchists see anarchism as a tool for creating just communities, aligning with Isaiah's vision of cities where righteousness dwells (Isaiah 58:12). They argue that rejecting hierarchical authority allows for the establishment of communities rooted in compassion, justice, and a commitment to addressing social issues.

10. **Resistance Against Oppressive Laws:**
   - Christian anarchists emphasize the need to resist oppressive laws and structures, aligning with Isaiah's call to "remove the yoke from among you, the pointing of the finger, the speaking of evil" (Isaiah 58:9). They argue that anarchism provides a

platform for challenging unjust laws and advocating for systemic change.

11. **Cultivating a Spirit of Solidarity:**
   - Anarchist principles, as advocated by Christian anarchists, cultivate a spirit of solidarity. They argue that rejecting hierarchical authority encourages individuals to stand in solidarity with those who are oppressed, echoing Isaiah's call for compassionate action.

12. **Vision for a Liberated Society:**
   - Christian anarchists envision a society liberated from oppressive structures, drawing inspiration from Isaiah's vision of a community that actively pursues justice, compassion, and the well-being of all. They argue that anarchism provides a framework for working towards this vision by actively resisting and transforming systems of injustice.

In summary, Christian anarchists draw from biblical critiques of injustice and oppression, such as Isaiah 58, to argue that anarchism provides a framework for actively resisting systemic injustice and working towards a more compassionate and equitable society. They see parallels between the biblical call for justice and the principles of anarchism in challenging hierarchical structures and promoting shared responsibility for the well-being of all.

45

Christian anarchists emphasize the inherent value of every individual as created in the image of God (Imago Dei). They argue that anarchism, which values the worth and dignity of each person, aligns with this fundamental biblical principle. Here's an exploration of this perspective:

1. **Imago Dei as the Basis of Human Dignity:**
   - Christian anarchists draw on the theological concept of Imago Dei, asserting that every individual is created in the image of God. This foundational belief underscores the inherent worth and dignity of each person,

irrespective of social status, ethnicity, or other characteristics.

2. **Anarchism's Embrace of Individual Worth:**
   - Advocates of Christian anarchism argue that anarchism, by rejecting hierarchical structures and coercion, inherently values the worth of each individual. They contend that an anarchist society promotes a respect for the unique qualities and intrinsic value of every person, aligning with the biblical principle of Imago Dei.

3. **Rejecting Dehumanizing Structures:**
   - Christian anarchists reject structures that dehumanize individuals, viewing such systems as incompatible with the Imago Dei. They argue that hierarchical and oppressive institutions can undermine the recognition of human dignity, and anarchism provides a framework for resisting and dismantling such structures.

4. **Equality in the Eyes of God:**

- Anarchist principles, according to Christian anarchists, uphold the equality of individuals in the eyes of God. They argue that anarchism challenges systems that perpetuate inequality and oppression, fostering an environment where everyone is recognized as equal before God and each other.

5. **Shared Responsibility for Human Flourishing:**
   - Christian anarchists contend that recognizing the Imago Dei compels believers to embrace shared responsibility for human flourishing. They argue that anarchism, by promoting mutual aid and cooperation, aligns with the biblical call to care for one another and ensures that each person has the opportunity to reach their full potential.

6. **Dismantling Discrimination and Prejudice:**
   - Advocates of Christian anarchism see anarchism as a tool for dismantling discriminatory structures and prejudices. They argue that recognizing the Imago Dei

necessitates challenging systems that marginalize certain groups, promoting a more inclusive and equitable society.

7. **Resisting Exploitation:**
   - Christian anarchists assert that recognizing the Imago Dei motivates resistance against systems that exploit individuals. They argue that anarchism provides a platform for challenging exploitative structures, fostering a society that values the well-being and dignity of all, in accordance with biblical principles.

8. **Encouraging Compassion and Empathy:**
   - Anarchist principles encourage compassion and empathy, according to Christian anarchists. They argue that recognizing the Imago Dei calls believers to extend love and understanding to one another, fostering a society where individuals care for the needs and concerns of their fellow human beings.

9. **Empowering Individuals:**

- Christian anarchists view anarchism as a means of empowering individuals. They argue that recognizing the Imago Dei implies empowering each person to actively participate in shaping their own destiny and contributing to the well-being of the community.

10. **Championing Individual Liberties:**
   - Advocates of Christian anarchism assert that anarchism champions individual liberties and autonomy. They argue that recognizing the Imago Dei involves respecting the freedom of each person to make choices, guided by their conscience and moral convictions.

11. **Celebrating Diversity:**
   - Christian anarchists celebrate diversity as an expression of the Imago Dei. They argue that anarchism fosters an inclusive society that embraces the diverse gifts, talents, and perspectives of individuals, enriching the community as a whole.

12. **Building a Community Grounded in Love:**
   - Christian anarchists envision a community grounded in love and mutual respect, reflecting the recognition of the Imago Dei. They argue that anarchism, by promoting voluntary cooperation and rejecting coercive authority, aligns with the biblical call to love one another as unique reflections of God's image.

In summary, Christian anarchists emphasize the inherent value of every individual as created in the image of God (Imago Dei). They argue that anarchism, which values the worth and dignity of each person, aligns with this fundamental biblical principle, promoting a society that respects human rights, rejects dehumanizing structures, and fosters equality and compassion.

46

Christian anarchists argue that by embracing anarchism, individuals actively participate in building a society that reflects the values of the Kingdom of God. They see anarchism as a way to bring about a more just and loving community in alignment with Jesus' teachings. Here's an exploration of this perspective:

1. **Kingdom of God Values:**
   - Christian anarchists draw inspiration from Jesus' teachings about the Kingdom of God. They argue that anarchism aligns with the values of love, justice, equality, and compassion promoted by Jesus as foundational elements of the Kingdom.

2. **Rejecting Earthly Hierarchies:**
   - Advocates of Christian anarchism contend that embracing anarchism involves rejecting earthly hierarchies and coercive structures. They argue that such rejection aligns with the Kingdom of God's principles, where God's reign is characterized by voluntary cooperation, love, and mutual respect.

3. **Embodying Jesus' Teachings:**
   - Christian anarchists see anarchism as a practical embodiment of Jesus' teachings.

They argue that the rejection of authoritarian structures and the embrace of voluntary cooperation mirror Jesus' emphasis on servant leadership, humility, and love for one another.

4. **Nonviolent Resistance to Injustice:**
   - Christian anarchists emphasize nonviolent resistance to injustice as a key aspect of Jesus' teachings. They argue that anarchism provides a framework for actively resisting oppressive systems without resorting to violence, aligning with the nonviolent principles of the Kingdom of God.

5. **Mutual Aid and Community Support:**
   - Advocates of Christian anarchism see anarchism as fostering mutual aid and community support, reflecting the communal values of the Kingdom of God. They argue that by prioritizing care for one another, individuals contribute to the establishment of a society that mirrors the supportive community envisioned in Jesus' teachings.

6. **Building a Culture of Love:**

- Christian anarchists view anarchism as a means of building a culture of love within society. They argue that the rejection of coercion and the promotion of voluntary cooperation create an environment where individuals can actively express love for their neighbors, aligning with the central message of Jesus.

7. **Dismantling Structural Injustice:**
   - Christian anarchists assert that anarchism involves actively dismantling structural injustice. They argue that by challenging hierarchical systems that perpetuate inequality, individuals contribute to the establishment of a society aligned with the Kingdom of God's vision of justice and equity.

8. **Creating Spaces for Inclusivity:**
   - Advocates of Christian anarchism argue that anarchism creates spaces for inclusivity. By rejecting oppressive structures, they contend that anarchism fosters a society where individuals from diverse backgrounds

are welcomed and valued, reflecting the inclusive nature of the Kingdom of God.

9. **Empowering Individuals to Serve:**
   - Christian anarchists see anarchism as empowering individuals to serve one another voluntarily. They argue that by emphasizing the importance of service over hierarchical authority, anarchism aligns with Jesus' teaching that the greatest among us is the one who serves others.

10. **Rejecting Earthly Kingship:**
   - Drawing from Jesus' rejection of earthly kingship during his temptation, Christian anarchists argue that anarchism aligns with the idea that God's Kingdom transcends worldly political structures. They contend that anarchism promotes a society where God's rule is recognized over human-made authorities.

11. **Creating Communities of Equals:**
   - Advocates of Christian anarchism envision anarchism as a way of creating communities of equals. They argue that by

rejecting hierarchical structures, individuals actively work toward building communities where everyone is valued and no one holds undue power, reflecting the egalitarian principles of the Kingdom of God.

12. **Living Out the Lord's Prayer:**
   - Christian anarchists see the practice of anarchism as living out the Lord's Prayer, particularly the phrase "Thy kingdom come, thy will be done, on earth as it is in heaven." They argue that anarchism aligns with the prayer for God's Kingdom values to be manifested in earthly communities.

In summary, Christian anarchists argue that embracing anarchism allows individuals to actively participate in building a society that reflects the values of the Kingdom of God. They see anarchism as a practical way to bring about a more just and loving community, in alignment with Jesus' teachings and the principles of the Kingdom of God.

Christian anarchists reject nationalism, drawing from the biblical call to love neighbors and enemies alike. They argue for a global perspective that transcends national boundaries, fostering solidarity and cooperation across borders. Here's an exploration of this perspective:

1. **Biblical Foundation of Love for Neighbors and Enemies:**
   - Christian anarchists root their rejection of nationalism in the biblical commandment to love neighbors and enemies alike (Matthew 5:43-48). They argue that nationalistic sentiments can undermine this fundamental principle of Christian ethics.

2. **Challenging Exclusive National Identity:**
   - Advocates of Christian anarchism contend that nationalism often fosters an exclusive national identity that may lead to discrimination against those outside the nation. They argue against any ideology that

hinders the extension of love and compassion to individuals beyond national borders.

3. **Global Solidarity as a Christian Principle:**
   - Christian anarchists promote global solidarity as a Christian principle, emphasizing the interconnectedness of humanity. They argue that a narrow focus on national interests can hinder the pursuit of justice, peace, and mutual aid on a global scale.

4. **Rejecting Tribalism and Xenophobia:**
   - Drawing from biblical teachings that discourage tribalism and xenophobia, Christian anarchists reject nationalism that fosters an "us versus them" mentality. They argue that such divisive attitudes contradict the inclusive love advocated by Jesus.

5. **Resisting Nationalistic Idolatry:**
   - Christian anarchists caution against the idolatry of the nation-state, arguing that elevating national identity to a position of ultimate importance may contradict the

biblical commandment to worship God alone. They emphasize the need to resist any form of idolatry that undermines Christian principles.

6. **Global Citizenship in the Kingdom of God:**
   - Advocates of Christian anarchism see themselves as global citizens in the Kingdom of God rather than prioritizing national identities. They argue that allegiance to a nation should not supersede the broader commitment to the principles of love, justice, and compassion promoted by Jesus.

7. **Promoting Peace Among Nations:**
   - Christian anarchists advocate for a global perspective that promotes peace among nations. They argue that nationalism, when taken to extremes, can contribute to conflict and hostility between nations, whereas a global perspective encourages collaboration and understanding.

8. **Rejecting the Use of Religion for Nationalistic Ends:**

- Christian anarchists reject the manipulation of religious beliefs to serve nationalistic ends. They argue against the co-opting of Christian faith for nationalistic agendas, emphasizing the importance of discerning between authentic religious values and political ideologies.

9. **Valuing Cultural Diversity:**
   - Christian anarchists appreciate and value cultural diversity without elevating one culture over another through nationalism. They argue for a celebration of cultural differences within the context of a global community that recognizes the dignity and worth of all individuals.

10. **Fostering Humanitarian Cooperation:**
   - Advocates of Christian anarchism emphasize humanitarian cooperation beyond national boundaries. They argue for a global approach to addressing issues such as poverty, inequality, and environmental challenges, recognizing the shared responsibility of humanity.

11. **Supporting Migrants and Refugees:**
   - Christian anarchists, drawing from biblical teachings on welcoming strangers and caring for refugees, argue against nationalistic policies that may contribute to the mistreatment of migrants. They emphasize the importance of compassion and hospitality toward those seeking refuge.

12. **Contributing to Global Justice and Equality:**
   - Christian anarchists advocate for actively contributing to global justice and equality. They argue that a rejection of nationalism allows individuals to work toward systemic changes that benefit all people, promoting a more just and equitable world.

In summary, Christian anarchists reject nationalism, drawing from the biblical call to love neighbors and enemies alike. They argue for a global perspective that transcends national boundaries, fostering solidarity, cooperation, and a commitment to universal Christian principles of love and justice.

48

Christian anarchists point to biblical examples of nonviolent resistance, such as Daniel's refusal to bow to the state's idol. They argue that an anarchist stance against coercion and violence aligns with these biblical examples of principled nonconformity. Here's an exploration of this perspective:

1. **Daniel's Nonviolent Resistance:**
   - Christian anarchists highlight the story of Daniel in the Bible, particularly the account in Daniel 3 where he refuses to bow down to the state's idol. Daniel's nonviolent resistance becomes a symbol of standing firm in one's convictions, even in the face of state coercion.

2. **Refusal to Compromise Faith:**
   - Advocates of Christian anarchism argue that Daniel's refusal to compromise his faith by bowing to the idol reflects a commitment to a higher authority, namely God. They see

this as an example of principled nonconformity to coercive state demands.

3. **Anarchism as Nonviolent Resistance:**
   - Christian anarchists assert that anarchism, as a rejection of coercive authority and hierarchical structures, is a form of nonviolent resistance. They argue that, like Daniel, individuals can resist unjust systems without resorting to violence, embodying principles of peace and justice.

4. **Rejection of State Coercion:**
   - Drawing parallels with Daniel's story, Christian anarchists reject state coercion and authority that goes against their principles of love, justice, and nonviolence. They argue that, like Daniel, individuals should resist conforming to oppressive state demands.

5. **Imitating Christ's Nonviolence:**
   - Christian anarchists connect the example of Daniel to Jesus' teachings on nonviolence. They argue that both Daniel's noncompliance and Jesus' call to turn the other cheek

exemplify a commitment to resisting injustice without resorting to violent means.

6. **Principled Opposition to Injustice:**
   - Advocates of Christian anarchism see Daniel's story as an illustration of principled opposition to injustice. They argue that anarchism provides a framework for individuals to resist and oppose coercive state actions while upholding ethical and moral principles.

7. **Refusing to Serve Multiple Masters:**
   - Christian anarchists draw from Jesus' teaching that one cannot serve both God and wealth (Matthew 6:24). They argue that Daniel's refusal to bow to the state's idol reflects a commitment to serve God alone, resisting the temptation to serve multiple masters, including the state.

8. **Anarchism as a Biblical Response to Oppression:**
   - Christian anarchists view anarchism as a biblical response to oppression. They argue that, like Daniel, individuals should resist

oppressive structures and systems that go against God's principles, seeking alternative ways to organize society based on justice and mutual aid.

9. **Defending Religious Freedom:**
   - Advocates of Christian anarchism emphasize the defense of religious freedom through nonviolent means. They argue that Daniel's story underscores the importance of standing up for one's faith without resorting to violence, advocating for a society where individuals can freely express their beliefs.

10. **Living Out the Prophetic Tradition:**
   - Christian anarchists connect Daniel's nonviolent resistance to the prophetic tradition in the Bible, where figures like Daniel, Isaiah, and Amos challenged oppressive powers. They argue that anarchism aligns with this tradition of speaking truth to power and resisting coercive authority.

11. **Rejecting Unjust Laws:**

- Christian anarchists argue for a rejection of unjust laws and practices. They draw inspiration from Daniel's nonconformity to state decrees that contradicted his faith, emphasizing the importance of resisting laws that go against higher ethical standards.

12. **Promoting a Kingdom-Centered Response:**
   - Advocates of Christian anarchism promote a Kingdom-centered response to societal issues. They argue that nonviolent resistance, inspired by biblical examples like Daniel's, aligns with the pursuit of a society grounded in the values of God's Kingdom, which includes justice, love, and nonviolence.

In summary, Christian anarchists point to biblical examples of nonviolent resistance, such as Daniel's refusal to bow to the state's idol, to argue that an anarchist stance against coercion and violence aligns with these biblical examples of principled nonconformity. They see these narratives as guiding principles for resisting injustice while upholding the values of love, justice, and faithfulness to a higher authority.

49

Christian anarchists advocate for community-based solutions to poverty, drawing from Jesus' teachings on caring for the least among us. They argue that localized, voluntary cooperation can address the root causes of poverty more effectively than top-down, state-driven approaches. Here's an exploration of this perspective:

1. **Jesus' Emphasis on Caring for the Poor:**
   - Christian anarchists begin with Jesus' explicit teachings on caring for the poor and marginalized, emphasizing passages like Matthew 25:31-46 where Jesus identifies himself with the hungry, thirsty, and those in need. They argue that addressing poverty is central to living out Christian principles.

2. **Voluntary Cooperation Over State Intervention:**

- Advocates of Christian anarchism argue against state-driven approaches to poverty, advocating instead for voluntary cooperation within communities. They believe that individuals voluntarily working together, without the imposition of external authority, aligns more closely with Jesus' teachings on compassion and care.

3. **Rejecting the Centralized State as the Solution:**
   - Christian anarchists reject the idea that a centralized state can effectively address the complexities of poverty. They argue that state-driven solutions often come with bureaucracy, inefficiencies, and unintended consequences, hindering the genuine, immediate care that communities can provide.

4. **Empowering Local Communities:**
   - Advocates emphasize the empowerment of local communities to take charge of addressing poverty within their midst. They argue that when communities are empowered to identify and respond to their unique needs,

the solutions are more tailored, sustainable, and rooted in a genuine concern for one another.

5. **Mutual Aid Networks as a Biblical Principle:**
   - Christian anarchists draw inspiration from biblical principles of mutual aid, where early Christian communities shared resources and cared for each other (Acts 2:44-47). They argue that such voluntary cooperation can be revived in modern times to effectively address poverty at the grassroots level.

6. **Creating Networks of Support:**
   - Christian anarchists envision creating networks of support within communities, where individuals voluntarily contribute time, resources, and expertise to uplift those experiencing poverty. They argue that such networks foster a sense of shared responsibility and communal care, in line with Jesus' teachings.

7. **Prioritizing Relationships Over Bureaucracy:**

- Advocates stress the importance of personal relationships in addressing poverty. They argue that community-based solutions prioritize direct, meaningful connections between individuals, fostering empathy, understanding, and a holistic approach to tackling the root causes of poverty.

8. **Resisting Dependence on the State:**
   - Christian anarchists resist the notion that dependence on the state is the solution to poverty. They argue that a reliance on state assistance can lead to disempowerment and perpetuate cycles of poverty, whereas communities taking the lead can foster self-sufficiency and dignity.

9. **Localized Knowledge and Solutions:**
   - Advocates highlight the importance of localized knowledge in understanding and addressing poverty. They argue that communities possess unique insights into the specific challenges their members face, and decentralized, community-driven solutions can respond more effectively to these nuances.

10. **Embracing Christian Principles of Love and Solidarity:**
   - Christian anarchists argue that community-based solutions to poverty align with Christian principles of love and solidarity. They see Jesus' emphasis on a personal, caring approach as a model for communities to emulate, fostering a sense of interconnectedness and shared responsibility.

11. **Fostering a Culture of Generosity:**
   - Advocates aim to foster a culture of generosity within communities, where individuals willingly contribute to the well-being of others. They argue that a voluntary, community-driven approach encourages a more generous and compassionate response to poverty.

12. **Building Resilient Communities:**
   - Christian anarchists envision community-based solutions as a way to build resilient communities that can collectively address challenges. They argue that fostering a spirit of cooperation and mutual support enables

communities to withstand crises and care for their vulnerable members effectively.

In summary, Christian anarchists advocate for community-based solutions to poverty, drawing from Jesus' teachings on caring for the least among us. They argue that localized, voluntary cooperation aligns more closely with Christian principles, emphasizing personal relationships, mutual aid, and shared responsibility as effective means of addressing the root causes of poverty.

50

Christian anarchists emphasize the biblical principle of embracing diversity and inclusivity. They argue that an anarchist society, which values the unique contributions of diverse individuals, aligns with the biblical vision of a community that transcends cultural, social, and ethnic boundaries. Here's an exploration of this perspective:

1. **God's Creation of Diverse Humanity:**

- Christian anarchists begin with the understanding that God created humanity in diverse forms, reflecting the richness of His creativity. They argue that recognizing and celebrating this diversity is a biblical principle rooted in the belief that every individual is made in the image of God.

2. **Inclusivity in God's Kingdom:**
   - Advocates of Christian anarchism point to the inclusivity found in the Kingdom of God as described in the Bible. They argue that an anarchist society, which values the contributions of all individuals irrespective of their backgrounds, aligns with the biblical vision of a diverse and inclusive community.

3. **Rejecting Discrimination and Exclusion:**
   - Christian anarchists reject any form of discrimination or exclusion based on cultural, social, or ethnic differences. They argue that embracing diversity is not only a moral imperative but also aligns with the teachings of Jesus, who emphasized love and inclusion.

4. **Jesus' Outreach to Marginalized Groups:**
   - Advocates draw from Jesus' ministry, highlighting His intentional outreach to marginalized and excluded groups. They argue that an anarchist society, mirroring Jesus' approach, actively seeks to include and uplift those often sidelined by societal structures.

5. **Anarchy as a Tool for Equality:**
   - Christian anarchists see anarchy as a tool for promoting equality and inclusivity. They argue that a society without hierarchical structures allows for the equitable participation of diverse individuals, fostering an environment where everyone's voice is heard and valued.

6. **Valuing Different Perspectives:**
   - Advocates stress the importance of valuing different perspectives within an anarchist framework. They argue that recognizing and appreciating diverse viewpoints leads to a more robust and

comprehensive understanding of societal issues, promoting collective wisdom.

7. **Biblical Call for Hospitality:**
   - Christian anarchists point to the biblical call for hospitality as a guiding principle. They argue that an anarchist society, marked by openness and hospitality, aligns with biblical values, creating a space where diverse individuals feel welcome and valued.

8. **Challenging Social Hierarchies:**
   - Advocates argue that anarchy challenges social hierarchies that often perpetuate exclusion and discrimination. They contend that dismantling hierarchical structures allows for a more equitable distribution of resources, opportunities, and recognition among diverse individuals.

9. **Community-Based Solutions for Inclusivity:**
   - Christian anarchists advocate for community-based solutions that actively promote inclusivity. They argue that localized, voluntary cooperation enables

communities to tailor their approaches to be culturally sensitive and inclusive, addressing the unique needs of diverse populations.

10. **Interconnectedness in the Body of Christ:**
   - Advocates draw parallels with the biblical metaphor of the Body of Christ, where diverse members work together for the common good (1 Corinthians 12:12-27). They argue that an anarchist society, recognizing the interconnectedness of individuals, reflects this biblical vision.

11. **Building Solidarity Across Differences:**
   - Christian anarchists envision an anarchist society as a platform for building solidarity across differences. They argue that fostering unity amidst diversity aligns with the biblical call to love one another and reflects the inclusive nature of God's love for all people.

12. **Anarchy as a Catalyst for Social Transformation:**

- Advocates argue that anarchy serves as a catalyst for social transformation, breaking down barriers and prejudices. They contend that embracing diversity within an anarchist framework contributes to the realization of a more just, loving, and inclusive society, in line with biblical principles.

In summary, Christian anarchists emphasize the biblical principle of embracing diversity and inclusivity. They argue that an anarchist society, which values the unique contributions of diverse individuals, aligns with the biblical vision of a community that transcends cultural, social, and ethnic boundaries.